Exorc... the Tree of Evil

By

William G Gray

Published by:

Kima Global Publishers
P.O. Box 374,
Rondebosch 7701,
Cape Town
South Africa

Telephone: +2721-686-7154
Fax: +2721-686-9066
E-mail: kima@global.co.za
Website: http://www.kimaglobal.co.za

ISBN 09584493-1-7

Previously published by Samuel Weiser 1974,

Second Edition 1984

This edition 2002

© Jacobus Swart 2003

Foreword

As a devoted "disciple" of William G. Gray, and being the "owner" of "Exorcising the Tree of Evil", I thought that this new edition 30 years after its initial publication, warrants a special introduction. Bill would not have liked me to refer to myself as his "disciple," but basically that is what I was for the fourteen years that I remained his student in Kabbalah, Magic, and the Western Mystery Tradition. Whilst recognising that I "got a lot" from William Gray, many "wesoterics" have asked why I am so devoted to him, and maybe the reason is best explained in his "Rite of Light": "Unbreakable are links of love which faith and friendship forge among all souls discerning one another by the Light within them."

Great as the heritage is that he passed in my direction, I believe the greatest legacy I received from him is the "Sangreal Sodality," a brotherhood engendered and born between us during one of his many visits to South Africa. If it is possible to summarize the basic stance of this tradition in one sentence, it would be: "If you seek your true Identity, and adjust yourself to fulfill the need Divinity *in you* has for Itself decreed, you will find the Grail of whom you truly are." Alternatively, as Credo Mutwa, the great Zulu medicine man once said to William Gray, "Man will never amount to anything until he knows who he is!" Of course this is much easier said than done, as all of us have at one time or another surrounded ourselves with the encrustations of the "pseudo-self," which we acquired when we "fell this far into flesh". By incarnating in this realm of manifestation, we have spawned our own "good" and "evil," both of which we will have to "exorcise" before we can reach any state of balanced self-hood, and claim ultimate union with the Eternal Living Spirit in whom we are ONE.

Yet, though the Quest may be tough indeed, and whilst it may take many lifetimes to see the slightest sign that we are getting nearer our goal, the important message Bill Gray wanted to impart is that we need to understand exactly whom we are, and then grow from that point using both mind and heart, i.e. find our ways to enlightenment between thinking and feeling. In the process we would have to deal with our "Devils within," which was ultimately personified as that grand fiend called "Satan," whose very name was used as a threat, and to bedevil the lives of millions. We all know how glibly the term "satanist" is slung at anyone marching to the beat of a different drum, or whose ideas of spiritual truth are not in agreement with those of the status quo. In this regard, occultists in particular have to put up with a lot of abuse. Yet, for all the "unspeakable practices" occultists of different types have been credited with, I do not believe any were ever as bad as the deliberate genetic engineers of modern day laboratories, who quite casually mix different genes so as to produce monstrosities and mutants.

Be that as it may, I personally do not believe in the existence of a literal Satan, since experience has shown that when an individual does something wonderful and good, the claim is: "That was me! I did that!" Yet, when that same individual commits an unacceptable act as far as society and his life are concerned, the exclamation is: "It wasn't me! It was the Devil who led me astray!" Refusing to take responsibility for ALL our actions, we blame the worst in ourselves, our own imperfections, on an entity visualized external to our own beings.

We also tend to blame the imperfections we find in life on the same entity, calling him "Satan" or the "Devil." Earthquakes, floods, and other natural disasters have either been viewed as punishments from God for the iniquities of the people, or they were brought on by the Devil. Yet, in ancient times there was an understanding that there were imperfections in God as well, as blasphemous as that may sound to the pious ears of fundamentalists. If all life is God, if there is nothing separate from Divinity, then all the imperfections we discover must also be God, and so it is largely correct to discover Its "imperfections" as far as Its immediate nature, i.e. that closest to humanity, is concerned.

Let us set aside the feelings of outrage at this blasphemy, so that we may understand what is being said. Life is a cycle, it never stops. Nobody is sort of wiped out, or sent to hell, against their free will, but sometimes individuals say: "I do not want to exist anymore. I have had enough." Of course free will is only relative to one's own evolution, but if someone suddenly decides not to *be* anymore, they start losing that autonomy. On the other hand it takes a lot more courage "to be." To go on in life is much harder than giving up altogether. It is so easy to say: "All right I am finished," or to put it in basic, crude language, it is like saying: "Okay God, reduce me to excrement!" and God obligingly does so. Yet, if people *really* want to throw themselves down the drain, that is their perfect right. It is the old story of "What doth it profit a man," etcetera. For example, many would gladly give their souls away for even the smell of money, and what is more, they have a perfect right to do just that.

So, looking at basics, we see that there is only *One* Supreme Being, Creative Consciousness, Life Force, or whatever you like to call "God," providing that your own, and everyone else's, genuine *raison d'etre is understood by that term. Now, that has to be an Energy, and energy implies a motion or exchange of force from one extremity to the other of the same "field." In other words, polarity or opposites in the sense of complementaries, as in the case of any force-phenomenon. To carry or extend the concept a shade further, we have the principles of "good" and "evil," personified as "God" and "Satan." If we postulate our concept of God as "Beneficence Personified," we necessarily imply Satan as "Malevolence Personified," but we should see not two beings but One expressed as alternative types of the same Energy, much as electricity is an active flow of particles between positive and negative polarities.*

To generate physical energy, we have to push material fuel *into* a body via the mouth, where part of it becomes converted into cell-supplies, with the rest reduced to rubbish and finally excreted as faeces and urine, which can still be useful to the ecology as fertilisers. Now, the *same process* takes place on spiritual levels of life, if we accept that we are really "made in God's image and likeness." To be brutally blunt, on those levels, "Satan" would serve the function of getting the excrement out of "God," or more accurately, keeping the metabolic balance of the Macrocosm in good order by evacuating *Its* "evil." That is why Satan was metaphorically seen in the past as the rear end of God, which literally gets rid of all the waste.

I believe we have been looking at things the wrong way for far too long in assuming a totally Beneficent God, who could not possibly be responsible for anything nasty or wrong in Its Creation. The key is in those vital words in Genesis 1:27 "So God created man in his own image, in the image of God created he him: male and female created he them." Later in Genesis 2 comes the corollary in verse 7 "And the Lord God formed man of the dust of the ground, and breathed into his nostrils the breath of life: and man became a living soul." There are two distinct accounts that form this creation myth, because Genesis is drawn from several original scrolls, but the im- plication of the first is quite clear that man is a replica of God to a minor extent, or at least conforms to the same principles. We are therefore to assume that, like our- selves, the Infinite consists of Living Energy, which in Itself is part of a process which we loosely call "Life." As such, *It* must have polarity and all that applies to this, plus we can only estimate the nature of *It* or *That* by extrapolating from ourselves accordingly, and filling in by guesswork, hopefully pointed in the right direction. So would it be asking too much to imagine a *vast Being with a Mind and a Mouth at one end from which only Good emerges, and an evacuating system at the other end which emits Evil? The good end we call God and the opposite end the Devil. Perhaps we might call the entire Being our GODEVIL. Can we imagine the "Good" end of It telling us via the Mind and Mouth how to dispose of Its Evil end? Is that too much to ask for? I think not.*

As far as things have been revealed to me, I can say with full conviction that this living Universe is worked by a polarised Power, one end of which we call "God" and the other "Satan". The God-end is like the Intelligence and finest feelings, but the Satan-end is the rear end so to speak. Fine so far. Now, if we are consumed by that Being, and we "go for the good end," we will evolve as expressions of Its behaviour, and identify with It until we pass altogether into a state of *Perfect Peace Profound,* and the "Mystical Marriage" is consummated. If, on the other hand, we choose the opposite end, or Satan, we have a wonderful time being "eaten" in order to supply fuel for the System, then reduced to residue, and ejected to pro- vide fertiliser for the Tree of Life, and here we go again with another Cosmic cycle.

If Satan is the rear end of God, you can hardly approach Divinity without dealing with the Devil can you? What about Isaiah 45:6-7 which reads: "I am the Lord and there is none beside me. I form the light, and create darkness. I make peace, and create evil. I the Lord do all these things." It is purely a question of dealing with the Devil *correctly*, in the way he *should* be dealt with. No more than that. What it all boils down to is "What do we want to become?" "Utterances" and "Words" coming out of the "Mind" and "Mouth" of God, or plain excreta out of Satan's behind. If "God" is the Being of which we all are parts as living creatures, and we are evolving through *It*, we can only exit from Its mouth or Its hind quarters. There are endless millions of humans who would rather become rejected excrement than face the onus of Godhood. So naturally they would want to worship Satan who gives them a short, good time, while gulping them down, so to speak, but the process of "Divine Gestation" is literally "hell," and that is the end of you as *you*. Those old legends of "selling yourself to the Devil" are literally true in one sense. Personifying the process did not make it any less accurate, providing you translated the terms into other levels of understanding.

Now, the concept that God might have anything to do with excrement horrified the Hebrews, because for some reason they were very puritanical about body waste, which they regarded as very disgraceful. However, the imperfections of God is a very old and arcane teaching, which of course the Christian Church rejected out of hand and invented the Devil instead to account for evil. Older esoterics saw God and Devil as only One Being, and it depended on which end of It you contacted as to what might happen. The crude image was that you either met God face to face when It kissed you fondly, or It presented the Satan end and covered you in excrement. This was one of the terrible secrets Kabbalists concealed beneath such a heap of euphemisms.

All of this is rather well indicated on the Tree of Life, where, if you fall into the upper Abyss, into the mouth of the Tree of Life as it were, you are going to go through the rectum of the Universe. Now, interestingly, while the "upper" Abyss is clearly indicated on the Tree of Life, the Lower Abyss at *Yesod* (Foundation) is never shown, and this is why there is a special "Archangel" or Genius of the Abyss called *Mesukiel* (Veiler of God), whose job was to conceal the imperfections of Divinity from humans, and presumably others, in the Abyss or *Mesak Mavdil* (Place of Rejected Failures). Nowadays we might call this a "Public Relations Officer"!

The "personal" part of "God" depends on us for Its process of perfection, just as we depend on the cells of our bodies to fulfill their functions properly so that we keep in good health and condition. In fact the relationship is an equivalent. Here you have to be careful and distinguish which part or aspect of God you experience. I am refer- ring here distinctly to the Logos. This Logos aspect is only that of *our* planetary system, while the Universal Aspect is that of *all* visible Creation, and behind that again *ad infinitum.*

I am reminded of that sentence in *"Western Inner Workings"*, in which William Gray maintained that "If I could get rid of my spiritual detritus as easily as I am voiding this physical waste, I might be in a better state of spiritual health altogether." By and large, I think we have lost a lot of information by being too "nice" in the past about basic facts of bodily behaviour, covering every- thing up as "shameful" purely because it dealt with our normal bodily functions.

Just as we cannot search for the benevolent God without also encountering the malevolent one, God forbid, we also cannot enter our own "secret souls" or those of others, seeking the "God-part" without also confronting the worst aspects. If you find the "God" in someone, you also have to encounter the "Devil" inside that person, and there are some nasty "Devils" twisted away in our Abysses which have not yet been eliminated. Some are more pathetic than vicious. Foolish maybe, some absurd, others laughable, a few quite nasty. Humans prefer their friends to meet only the "best Sunday go to meeting" side of themselves, and keep their "devils" out of the way. Quite right too, but it is only to one's very intimate Spiritual Companions, that one dares reveal that darkest side of an inner character. Only the strongest and most genuine Inner ties can possibly survive an encounter with a stark naked human soul.

This and a lot more is part of what William Gray addressed in a most practical manner in "Exorcising the Tree of Evil." In clear and unmistakable terms he tells us that we shall not rid our world of any evils, social or otherwise, unless we address their origins within our own beings. All the problems we have to deal with in life begins and ends within us. It is our the task to regenerate our own unregenerate natures, and in this remarkable book we are told exactly how to transmute the worst and the best inside ourselves in our quest for Godhood.

Jacobus G. Swart

Johannesburg 2003

Table of Contents

Chapter One

Polarity

Polarity *per se*, is not only a normal fact of life in this world, but is also a necessity for evolution. Our continual struggle against every form of adversity has advanced all our forms of civilization and culture. By itself it is neither good nor bad, but just an essential of existence, especially if we intend to develop ourselves as spiritual beings. We need the battle between good and evil presented in specific quantities and qualities so that it will correct and compensate for all our shortcomings as creatures of consciousness intent on the improvement of our souls. In other words, it has to be a suitable "battle" for each individual case.

It was a very old theory that God created the Devil for the particular purpose of functioning as the spiritual adversary of mankind. His job was to test and try us with every kind of "temptation" to go wrong and divert us from the direct path to divine perfection. Our resistance to these urges and correct reactions with them would build up enough spiritual strength and integrity to take us right to the top of the Tree of Life. Though this may not be literally true, it is a good plan to live as if it were, which is also true of many religious myths.

Once we think of anything as "good", we have to perceive the possibilities of "evil" as well. Esoteric legendry is full of our fabled "fall" which occurred when we began to distinguish between opposing energies of the life-principle. By contrasting courses of conduct and effects of the energies operating through them, we came to know their differences-terming one end *good*, and the other *evil*. So far as humans were concerned one was apparently beneficial, while the other was maleficent. Things were as simple as that in those far-off days. All current complications are due to our dealings with them since those times.

The basic facts of this matter are that energy can be classified as polarized power with a positive (+) and a negative (-) nature; the flow of force from one pole to the other constitutes its effective action. A consistent balance between them, when each is exactly equal to the other, results in a state of perfect neutrality or "power at peace". It would be a sad mistake to confuse the principles of good and evil with the poles of + and -, because each is a polarised manifestation of life-energy, with a + and _ of its own, while the principle of adversity can be a combination of both or a concentration of either. By itself it is neither, being nothing more or less than a law of life in its own right.

Unhappily, we have come to associate the principle of adversity with that of evil alone, and many Westerners also link the polarity of negative with both exclusively. Ever since *The Power of Positive Thinking* was written, an absolute phobia has arisen concerning what is presumed to be "negative thought". People have been pre-conditioned to the presumption that if they want to "think successful" they will automatically attract to themselves whatever they think about. If they want to be rich they must "think riches". If they want to be popular they must think everybody loves them and so on. Under no circumstances must they ever imagine anything evil or adverse ever happening to them. All they have to do is keep visualizing "positive prosperity" – and it will be theirs. Somehow they identify the term "negative" with all that is bad and undesirable, while the word "positive" means what- ever may be good and pleasant. This completely erroneous association of words with values has probably caused more confusion than many other man-made mistakes.

It should surely be obvious to any thinking person that the principles of good and evil must apply to both ends of the moral scale or neither. There can no more be a positive without a negative to match it than there can be a good without an evil, by inference alone. Therefore the idea of "think only positive thoughts" is just as silly as trying to pick up one end of a stick without the other end accompanying it. *There is a positive and a negative good, just as there is a positive and a negative evil.* The ideal condition to hope for would be one wherein both principles balanced each other out perfectly and thus resulted in a state of harmony throughout the whole.

One of the first laws learned in the study of electro- magnetism is: Like poles repel, unlike poles attract. There- fore there could be an adequate case made for the theory that prolonged concentration on either polarity would automatically attract its opposite. It would not be a good idea to dwell on either exclusively without acknowledging the existence of its opposite. This does not imply that for every intended act of *good* there should be an intended act of *evil* to balance it, or vice versa. That would not only be a wrong interpretation in itself, but be self-defeating in addition. What it means is that a deliberate choice between two known courses should be made by consciously contrasting them, and ultimately a *middle way of balance* be chosen and put into practice.

It must never be forgotten that the terms good and evil are purely our human interpretations of energy-effects in relation to our lives. This is of paramount importance, and if we lose sight of that we shall never be able to relate ourselves properly with either polarity. The old adage, "One man's meat is another man's poison," could also be read as, "One man's good is another man's evil". Classification depends entirely on estimation. Nevertheless, over the centuries of human civilization we have man- aged to classify a great deal of activity and behaviour into recognisable categories which the majority of mankind agrees may be termed as good, evil, or simply indifferent. Most of us have the hereditary basics of these implanted in our genes, but there are notable exceptions.

There are beings in human bodies who see no more wrong in murdering some helpless victim for personal pleasure or profit than a cat sees anything wrong with killing a mouse. These cannot exactly be classed as evil in themselves, though they are indeed dangerous to the community at large and should be treated as such. Even more dangerous are those that recognise evil for what it is, yet adopt its courses deliberately and skillfully in order to gain some material advantages in this world. Most dangerous of all are the relatively few who know evil for exactly what it is and exploit it scientifically on spiritual levels for the promotion of their own power and preferred positions. These could indeed be called black magicians in every sense of the term.

Once they adopt the creed of "evil – be thou my good", they become totally committed to the cause of evil for its own sake and ends. Fortunately for humanity as a whole, such souls are even more uncommon that those who devote themselves to either extremity is a very unwise choice in life, resulting in serious soul-problems of unbalance. Moreover, the more we evolve the more complicated do our form of good and evil change and adapt with our development. The tendency is for these to become increasingly alike in external appearance so that they are very difficult to distinguish from each other in essence.

The legend of the original Edenic Tree* was that it gave humans the ability to know the difference between good and evil. That is to say we became consciously and instinctively aware that there were right and wrong ways of living if we intended to perfect ourselves as a life-species. It was not that we realized the precise whys, whats, and hows of all the moral issues involved, but simply that a difference existed between life-methods which could be classified as "right" or "wrong" been arguing and quarrelling about acceptable codes of behaviour in relation to our discoveries.

What humanity was trying to do at that point was develop a spiritual life along the same biological principles as a physical existence. The first thing a fertilized egg does is divide into a bi-part being. Thenceforth life becomes a matter of subdivision and specialization until the finished product appears as a sexually polarized creature which will eventually be able to initiate the process all over again, and so *ad infinitum*. Here we can trace our fabled "fall" to the dawnings of conscience in the human race when the fruit of the Tree of Knowledge enabled us to distinguish between the Tree of Life and its opposite Tree of Evil as the dark shadow thrown by the light of experience. Once we realized there was a good and a bad side to living in this world – and the choice of either lay in our own hands – evolution altered entirely. Figuratively we had crossed the abyss on spiritual levels and begun building downwards.

19

Look at the standard Tree of Life pattern in Figure 1 on page 20. From the pure *consciousness* of Sphere 1, we come to an awareness of *right* at 2, *wrong* at 3, then via the *Bridge of Knowledge* across the abyss to a lower-level resultant of *Mercy* at 4 and *Severity* at 5. We need *Mercy* to encourage right and *Severity* to deter wrong. Projecting further towards matter these harmonize at Sphere 6, *Balanced Beauty*. From that point, consciousness divides again into the dual *concepts of Victory* at Sphere 7 and *Glory* at Sphere 8. This seems to indicate that while it is "right" to seek victories in life-situations, it would be "wrong" to gain glory or self-satisfaction from them. So stabilization is sought again at the central 9th Sphere position of *Foundation*, and then everything is ready for final projection into the *material kingdom of this world* at Sphere 10.

Notice the sequence is that of 1, know something; 2, do something; and 3, abstain from something. Know, act, don't act. Know what to do, then what not to do, and then combine both in order to decide direction. That is the rule advised by the Tree of Life. Reading down the left pillar of the Tree, wrong can be known by *understanding*, con- trolled by *severity*, and averted by *honour*. Conversely, right may be known by *wisdom*, extended by *compassion*, and consolidated by *victory*. First awareness, then out- going activity, lastly curtailment of energy. Such is the cycle of Life in terms of the Tree.

It will probably be noticed also, that the principles of wrong becomes equated with the left, or feminine, side of the Tree – which will naturally be resented by every reasonable woman on earth. This certainly does not mean that any woman is evil *per se*, but it does indicate that the essential feminine element of humanity has the unique function of understanding, controlling, and averting those wrongs and evils which plague us in this world.

Polarity

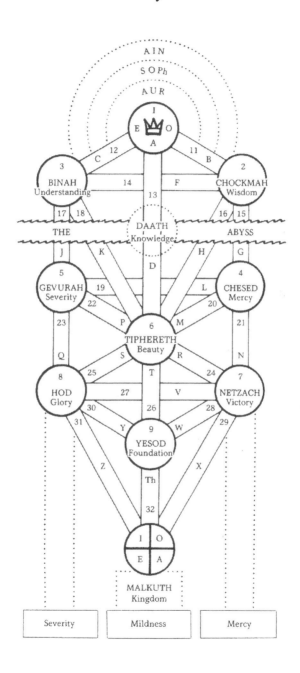

If the mission of man should be to do good, then surely the mission of woman is to prevent or abnegate evil? She begins this by controlling her own behaviour, then influencing her husband's and children's. After that – extension past the home into the wider world. The effect of women as abaters and preventers of evil everywhere is incalculable. Eve is seen here as the redeemer of Adam. Unhappily it is also true to say that when they go wrong and actively or passively encourage evil, the results are correspondingly frightening. A weak man and a wicked woman in partnership is a tragedy to be deplored more than most. So also is that of a wicked man with a woman too weak to avert or at least deflect his evil intentions.

Looking at the other pillar of the Tree on the right or "good" side, it should be self-evident that if impulses were not directed by the qualities of wisdom and knowledge, results could be disastrous. Those are prerequisites before the energy is converted to further action. Unwise good can have very ill effects as many have learned by sad experience. It is never enough to *intend good* alone unless the subsequent action is directed and backed by adequate knowledge. For ex- ample, in the event of an accident wrong attempts at first-aid could easily kill or injure the victim even further, no matter how good the intentions of would be helpers were.

Once the idea of an Adverse Tree of Evil had come from the notion of a dark and shadowy Tree appearing in contrast to the Tree of Life illuminated by the light of truth, it was only natural to explain its design in terms of reversed ideology. If evil is the opposite of good, then there has to be some kind of an "opposite number" to God. So the concept of a head spirit of evil was identified under various titles, most of them signifying an adversary or opposer. Some- thing in the nature of an anti-God which worked against the will and intentions of the Deity, was totally opposed to all the workings of that divine will in mankind. Since each sphere on the Tree of Life had some specific god-aspect and operative archangel attributed to its significance, it became necessary to postulate a set of corresponding evil spirits for their own counter-Tree. Eventually an acceptable and plausible collection were suggested as follows:

Sphere 1 has a combination of both Satan and Moloch for joint rulership. Satan as the adversary-concept, and Moloch as a consumer of child life or destructor of humanity before it was able to reproduce its species. The old picture of Moloch as an idol build around a furnace into which living children were thrown gives some idea of ancient practices connected with drastic population control by enforced extinction. Perhaps the crematoria in wartime prison camps for the disposal of Jewish bodies might be considered as a modern equivalent. Moloch may be seen in many forms. The order of lesser demons listed here is that of the Thamiel. The suffix "el" signifies "of God", and indicates that evil angels were only allowed to operate by permission of the deity. This particular genus of malignancy means closer-up or finisher, which seems appropriate for this terminal position on the Tree.

Sphere 2 has Beelzebub for a demonic lord. Literally the "Lord of the Flies". Originally a god-aspect appealed to against plagues of the pests, but afterwards considered as a deity devil invoked to inflict such a type of evil on enemies. He was associated with diseases and pestilence. For his assistant he had Chaigidel, or "Life-cutter of God", an instigator of multiple minor injuries which eventually total to major proportions. Very often a prolonged and continual series of small injuries can do more damage to humans than a single calamitous event of great significance.

Sphere 3 is credited with the Archdemon Lucifuge, which is a Latin term meaning "One who flies from the Light". Since the third Sphere on the Tree is that of understanding, it is easy to see how this evil genius signifies whatever avoids the clear light of comprehension anywhere. One might see Lucifuge as being an encourager of those who refuse to understand anything and prefer to live in deliberate ignorance. His coadjutor is named as Satariel, which seems to derive from roots indicating one who hides or covers up secret sins. Otherwise a refusal to recognize sins or wrongs in oneself.

Sphere 4 once the Abyss of Ignorance is crossed, has an anti-deity named Astaroth, a plural term for flocks, crowds or assemblies. It was also the name of the Goddess Astarte much hated by the Hebrews for her sexual proclivities. She was worshipped with acts of licentiousness and prostitution in old Phoenicia. Her partner in crime, Gamchicoth, connects with "Those that are crooked or bent", a phrase still in current use to indicate dishonesty and untrustworthiness.

Sphere 5 is ruled by Asmodeus, the destroyer or exterminator. There is a legend that he was the result of incest between Tubal-Cain and his sister Naamah, and therefore represents extreme impurity. His principle assistant Galab has the odd significance of a barber, but the shaver-off-of-beards was an old euphemism for a depriver of manhood or a castrator. The loss of a beard was usually equated with sexual impotence, and that is the unspoken threat implied here.

Sphere 6 has Belphegor as its anti-God. The prefix Bel or Baal only signifies "chief", or "headman". This one was once worshipped by the Moabites on Mount Phegor which means a corpse. His name would therefore stand for a ruler of corpses or "King of the Dead". His partner Tagarim has a connotation with flaying or laying bare to the bone, and the word is a masculine plural, so we have here a combination of death-dealers on a most unpleasant scale.

Sphere 7's evil genius is simply called Baal – an overlord. It was a title rather than a specific name and probably indicates what we would now call "the establishment" as a term of dislike for ruling politicians. Perhaps we might translate the title as "bad government". His helper, Hareb Serapel, is signified by a multiplicity of those kindling a funeral pyre. So here we have a connection with death and destruction through faulty and corrupt control of government.

Sphere 8 is ruled by an evil entity named Addramalech. He is supposed to be the Chancellor of Hell, and was once a local deity worshipped in Abyssinia where children were burned on his altar. Sometimes he was seen as a mule and sometimes as a peacock, which bird represents the devil for the Yezidi sect on account of its symbolic pride. So Addramelech seems to be a combination of stubbornness and vanity. His adjutant Samael means "Venom of God", or spiritual poisons of any sort, such as venomous speech or toxic thought.

Sphere 9 has Lilith, the female Fiend, for its anti-Deity. She was reputed to be the first wife of Adam who bore him nothing except devils and monstrosities. She is regarded as "Queen of the Succubi" and mistress of miscarriages. On spiritual levels she tries to abort all the best ideas and intentions of mankind. Her assistant is Gamaliel, stemming from a root meaning something to bear in the nature of a burden, so we have the impression of some unpleasant imposition upon mankind.

Sphere 10 has another female Devil known as Nahema. To moan and groan as if at a funeral. There may have been a thought here to connect this with a nagging woman as a common infliction to be encountered on earth, but it is meant to indicate what a world of wailing and grief awaits the wicked. Just plain misery everywhere. Her partners are simply called Nahemoth, those that help carry out this gloomy process.

There have been a fairly comprehensive picture of what old time Qabbalists imagined would be the staffing personnel of a Tree of Evil, whose duties would consist of tempting or threatening humanity away from the straight and narrow path of righteousness which led centrally up the Tree of Life from earth to Heaven. It may be a coincidence that Norse myth- ology visualized a Hell below the Earth among the roots of their Earth-Tree where evilly inclined individuals would expiate their guilt in an icy desolation of lonely misery. Qabbalists did not see such a specific Hell at all, but saw lost souls as leaves which had fallen off the Tree of Life and became reduced to humus which eventually mingled with the soil to promote new growth. A hell wherein fiends tortured damned souls for no other purpose than their won amusement seemed utterly fruitless and waste ful to practical Qabbalists. They considered their demons to be agencies that handled the break-down process of katabolism and reduced the effete elements of life to their lowest possible basics prior to the reabsorption of those atoms into the anabolic or "build-up" side of creation which was operated by angels.

It is an old adage that no one is ever tempted past their power to bear, and for every type of evil entity there is a corresponding angel of light to counter its influence. All any informed human had to do was call clearly enough for the appropriate celestial aid. Consequently long lists were made of demonic and angelic names or identifications of opposing energies which constituted the goods and bads of most human situations. Once the bad was identified, then the correct good might be summoned up to deal with it. It was most important to know which exact name to use, or the magic would be ineffective. Conversely, in the case of black magic, it was necessary to know precisely which specific demon to invoke for working the type of evil required. Generalisations were considered insufficient, and wrong attributions were liable to cause more damage to the employer than the objective. The psychology of this is very interesting.

If human consciousness becomes aware of good and evil, that means it is capable of polarization or distinction between opposites. In fact it is primarily the perception of contrast alone that makes objective consciousness possible. We perceive everything by our awareness of contrast and estimate anything by distinguishing it from all else that it is not. All our senses work that way. Our vision sees the differences between light and darkness. Our hearing reacts to the difference between sounds and silence. Our touch responds to distinction between variations of contact-pressures or absence of them. Our inner senses follow the same laws and distinguish between principles wherever they have polarities. It is the story of the Tree every time. Right, left and centre; positive, negative and neutral; good, bad and indifferent.

It figures that the sharper and more detailed conscious awareness of anything becomes, the keener will be the percipients sense of its identity. Our method of classifying this is by means of words or sonic symbols which cover its nature for us as completely as possible. If a single word is inadequate then a combination of words have to be used, and preferably as few as possible. That was why the Tree consisted of *primal principles*, each of which could then be divided into polarities of good and evil by contrast of properties, then typifying these again by God or Devil name, and subsequently defining ever more closely and finely by employing specific names for "spirits" to describe detailed points of its nature until the greatest awareness of its identity is reached.

Nowadays of course, we can see this process as a method of reaching a required result by following a line of "yes or "no" options until no further progress is possible, and thus arrive at the most accurate average for all practical purposes. By working out appropriate terminology for angels and demons alike, Qabbalists and their associates hoped to find "condensers of consciousness" which would make the most effective foci for the forces of their feelings and their thinking. Thus they hoped would the word actually become the deed, and what they said meaningfully would actually happen on every level of life including this material one. What they said with *will* could be made manifest through *meaning*.

This idea of materializing concepts into actualities by the medium of words was a fundamental of magic, both black and white. In principle it is quite true. We do have to arrange our consciousness in terms of verbalizations and numeral values so that an ultimate resultant can be constructed on physical levels, presuming we want to condense it that far. In order to make anything manifest on earth, we have to process it through a whole collection of figures and words before it appears in material form.

Think of the amazing arrangement of words and figures that preceded our first or any subsequent flight to the moon. Then consider our most modern type of magic, computes and word processors. All of these are direct descendents of ancient thought processing, traceable back to esoteric sources when advanced humans began to classify consciousness itself into a methodology of thinking by combining thought values with number values. When human literacy married human numeracy our real civilization began.

It may be remembered that Qabbalists posited a four-fold process of thought-development. First origination where ideation commenced, then creation where it developed. Later formation where it matured, and finally expression where it actually appeared amongst mankind. They called these stages the *four worlds*, and their theory is just as valid now as it was then. It applied to both good and evil thinking alike, but we have the ability to negate it at any stage prior to the last. For example, how many people get urges to murder someone, plan everything down to the last detail, then call it off at the last moment? There are probably millions of such incidents, and the same applies with most other forms of crime or violence.

Conversely, there must be an equivalent amount of beneficial ideas envisaged to the same degree yet never actuating on earth. All these unmaterialized thoughts are like the millions of sperm cells which never find an egg and eventually become another human being. Again we have the yes or no factor in action. An idea is originated, then immediately comes the question of whether or not to let it continue into the next stage and be developed creatively. Frequently it is stopped right there and is negated back to zero again. Should it develop in the creative stage, the yes or no barrier comes up again at the edge of the formative world, and if it is allowed to be formed as far as possible, the final check point is met with immediately before projection into this expressive world, and that is the decision which has to be made by the ideating individual.

It does not follow that once the idea appears on earth it would accomplish anything in particular. Thousands of factors might abort, alter, or even suppress it entirely. Once materialized, it becomes vulnerable to the ideation of other humans. Up to its entry point in this world, an idea is under the control of its creator, but the moment it materializes it encounters the consciousness of others which may influence it in multiple ways. It is no longer private property but becomes part of our communal consciousness to whatever degree humans are willing or able to share it. Therefore those who seek control over their own consciousness and behaviour should start by asking themselves a lot of questions.

"How far do I want to develop my thinking? Is it worth bringing to the creative stage? If not, then I must push it back into negation. Shall I bring it as far as the formative stage? Do I want to bring any of this into my objective living, and if so how much of it?" Once the decision has been taken to materialize the idea in some way, definite action must then be taken. Such action may fail, be ineffective, or even be entirely useless. That is not important. What matters is that some conscious and intentional effort be made in physical terms to bridge the gap between the worlds of formation and expression.

This initial act of materializing thought need not be anything very spectacular or arduous by itself. It could be anything from making a note on a piece of paper to performing quite an elaborate ritual. So long as it is enough to actually *express* the ideology in some form of recognizable earth-appearance, that will be sufficient to supply its "toe-hold" so to speak in our dimensions of life. The rest will follow according to expenditures of time and energy devoted to its development. Such was the purpose of talismans, conjurations, and all the physical appurtenances of old-time magic. They acted as physical terminals for lines of thought coming from very remote origins.

To some degree this may seem like the catching of a grapnel on the edge of something to be scaled first by a single climber, then by others up the more substantial ladders he is able to emplace for them, and after that by many along the solid road they are able to construct together. The "thin edge of the wedge" or pioneering process. This is exactly what it is in spiritual terms. An actual contact on material levels which opens the way for a further flow of the potential energy produced by all their previous work on preceding levels. Obviously the better this is accomplished the finer will be the flow, but should it be unsatisfactory or careless, no material efficacy may be expected. The importance of adequate work on the first three levels of consciousness prior to projecting it into material manifestation can scarcely be overstressed.

Of course a great deal of inner energy is not intended to come very far into materialisation. The ultimate expression of an idea on our levels may only work out as casual conversation or in relatively trivial ways. It could be confined to the experience of a single individual or propagated through some media whereby millions of minds could share it. What we are concerned with here is the actual workings of the process and how we might alter the angles of adversity by study of its patterns as seen against the Tree of Life design.

It seems quite obvious that unless we tackle the problems of evil and adversity both consciously and intentionally in this world, we shall eventually be destroyed by our own creations. Actually the same result would happen if humans decided to devote themselves exclusively to good, though in an entirely different way. What we need most is a careful control of both pro- pensities until we are able to live as sane and balanced people capable of regulating our conduct in all our worlds of existence. We shall certainly not do this by pretending that evil does not exist or equating it with negation and deluding ourselves that "thinking positively" is the answer to all our problems. All that would do is create a fool's paradise which could collapse like a house of cards when hit by very active evil coming round the corner.

We need to *know* and recognize evil very clearly indeed in order to obviate its insidious influence and eventually eliminate its effects on this earth. We can only do that by changing its character - which begins with changing our own. We may know what good and evil are in theory, but their forms and application are altering so much during the centuries that they are becoming increasingly difficult to distinguish from each other. Obvious adversities are still clear enough, but the dividing line between them and their opposites is becoming more and more obscured over the passage of relatively fewer years. Confronted by such confusion, what are baffled humans supposed to do?

The code of conduct is the same now as it always was, no matter how methods may have changed. *Alter a positive evil into a negative good, then neutralize* it. *Likewise alter a negative evil into a positive good and then neutralise that.* Note that the aim is always the centralization of energy as a balance between both principles. Qabbalists call this the *Middle Pillar Practice* and extol it as the ideal way of living in line with light. Note especially the dir- ection of circulation. From evil towards good, then into neutral and back to evil again. A constant stirring of life-energy from one polarity to another in an ever- advancing direction towards *divinity.* It is actually the intention which we can alter of our own accord. Once the evil is present in this world it has to be worked out or mitigated as best we can, but by altering our attitudes towards it a great deal can be changed into more favourable forms of experience though seldom as rapidly as might be wished. By such alterations on inner and intentional levels, a very practical contribution to the welfare of this world will have been made.

This was the reason that Jesus advised his followers to take the then novel course of returning good for evil, or al- tering the nature of received adverse energy. Had he made it clear that both were bi-polar energies and needed to be dealt with accordingly, it might have been more helpful. We have to understand exactly what the poles of evil are, and how they bring adversity to us. Its positive nature is when directed energy is emitted with the inten- tion of damaging or injuring conscious creatures in any way that causes their physical or spiritual deterioration. Its negative nature evidences as deprival of beneficial influences, prevention of development, encouragement of inherently bad qualities, or obviating good which might otherwise have been done. In other words, the positive side of evil is when it is aimed at anyone or at larger targets by another source of intention, and its negative nature is aimed at bringing inherent evils out of people or from any other possibility. Since like poles repel, a positive evil is best countered by a positive good, and a negative evil by a negative' good.

In general terms the definition of positive (+) in relation to its source is of emission or outputting, while that of negative (-) is one of admission or intaking. What a source puts out as a positive polarity of energy has to be taken in or admitted somewhere by a negative nature. Thus a positive evil would be most attracted by a negative good and vice versa. Therefore the ideal life-attitude to adopt as a normal condition would be one of negative evil in oneself so as to attract positive good from elsewhere, and a positive good in oneself so as to attract negative evil in return. If such a state can be reached and maintained, maximum benefits and minimum adversities should certainly result.

Because the basic direction behind both good and evil is *intention,* they have to be traceable to some source of intelligence or guiding consciousness, whether human or otherwise. The vast majority of either we encounter in this world is of human origin, but that does not exclude the operations of other intelligences working along spiritual lines of communication. The old and simplistic method of considering these was by postulating "God" as a spirit of *entitised energy* who only employed good, and his opposite "Satan" the *adversary* who directed nothing but evil. We may have grown beyond this belief as a literal statement, but it could still be a useful one as a theorem for dealing with the problem in practice. By controlling our conduct *as if* God and Satan were actualities, we should also arrange ourselves into practical patterns of power aimed at accomplishing our own perfection.

For example, if in the grip of some particular type of thought-current, it would always be wise to inquire its origins and nature. Does it originate in oneself or elsewhere? From G or the devil? Good or evil and which polarity? What is important is that an honest attempt at analysis should be made whether 1 results turn out to be right or wrong. Such is all part of the control of consciousness which marks the difference between those who intend to make meaning out of their lives and the vast majority of humans who just drift from one damaging experience the next without putting up much, if any, resistance.

Factually, it is our efforts against all the adversities we encounter in life which has made us what we are at present. , may be over-familiar with the phrase: "battle of life," but that what it truly amounts to. A constant struggle against all the ma forces that threaten human survival and spiritual status. At first the forces of nature themselves, and now the much more malignant forces from within ourselves and those directed at us from anti-human intelligence. Dealing with nature was relatively easy compared to the formidable battle ahead of us in dealing with human and other agencies of malignancy among us. The only certainty of this issue is that unless we succeed in winning the most important battle for our being-hood, we shall definitely be destroyed.

It may be a source of wonderment to many elderly people why youngsters look for "causes" to defend or pursue devotedly. Some of these "causes" seem so pointless or even sane, yet the necessity for them *per se* cannot be denied. They provide opportunities for a prac- tice at spiritual struggling, which exercises and promotes soul-growth in the individuals concerned. It is the equivalent of young animals having mock-batt with each other in order to develop latent inherited life-abilities for hunting and surviving. The tragedy comes among humans when this turns to terrorism and wars which are so coldly exploited by older people who know very well how to extract, political and commercial profit from the unnecessary deaths a ruin of countless human lives.

As previously noted; the first major battle in life emergence from a womb. That is often a long and bitter struggle: involving an exhausting expenditure of energy for both mother and baby alike. Later in life comes puberty with the first emergence into adulthood. This is when we feel most vulnerable and surrounded by hostile forces opposing our entry into the world of social activities. Our instincts are to gather with our peers, identify the hostile elements if we can, then fight them as best we may. On worst levels this means physical war- fare, and best, spiritual conflict with whatever we feel should be resisted or altered for the better. These instincts are inbred so deeply in our genetics that they can neither be denied nor avoided. The only sensible thing to do is channel them as correctly as can, make the best use of expended energy and hope for results in terms of spiritual development.

What matters most is that youngsters should see and understand this point consciously and clearly. They should realize it is natural and normal for them to oppose all they believe to be evil earth. What they really need most is a reliable working methodology for accomplishing this in the most effective way. Instead of descending to violence and terrorism which only result in arousing hatred, fear and antagonism from other humans, let them employ the more practical if less dramatic methods of "attitude altering" streams of consciousness directed intelligently against what they regard as "the opposition." The concentration and efforts needed to do this will result in the needed self-improvement they are instinctively seeking on inner levels.

It could be that the Christian church realized this when they invented their version of the adversary-spirit as "the devil," and 'personalized the' 'powers of darkness" into the shape of beings epitomizing every evil, thus challenging all mankind to the battle life with individual immortality as the stakes to win or lose. Summoning up everything of a similar nature and giving it a generic name is quite a practical way of tackling whatever it may by providing a focal point of consciousness. Offering "the devil" as an antagonist to fight on spiritual levels instead of .fighting each other on earth physically was a hopeful method of 'persuading people to become peaceful allies instead of political enemies. Even though it did not work like that, the idea was a well-meant one, and the principle holds possibilities for the future.

Most religions postulated anti-human spiritual beings of some kind who manipulated energies calculated to have adverse effects on humanity. Possibly one of the most sophisticated versions was the Qabbalistic legend that Satan was an archangel specifically charged by God to offer opportunities of evil to mankind, thus affording us the needed adversity to fight and consequently gain further advancement of spiritual status for selves. The tale goes on with the story that every time any human falls for temptation and commits an evil act, Satan sheds a tear, because this condemns him also to its consequences al prolongs his stay in hell just that much more. It means that only when and if the whole of humanity rejects evil forever will Satin be freed from his miserable occupation and allowed to live light eternally with the rest of us. As things are at present, it looks as if the unhappy Spirit of Evil is faced with a long term office yet.

We are not in this world to ignore evil and adversity, but *know,* understand, and *deal* with it. This makes for a major distinction between the Oriental inner tradition and our ow Generally the Eastern viewpoint is to deplore evil while at t. same time trying to avoid, rise above, avert, or keep out of cc tact with it as far as possible. The Western attitude, on the other hand, is to come to grips with evil on its own ground and defeat it by every possible means. The Eastern belief is that evil or exists on the lowest planes of existence, therefore it is best to advance oneself spiritually beyond these as rapidly as evolution, allows, so arriving at a state of heaven and beyond it to that nirvana where; "The wicked cease from troubling and the weary are at rest."

A Salvation Army captain once put it a little differently when she said: "I suppose you think that we all want to go to heaven when we die? Well we don't. The ambition of every true Salvationist, is to get into Hell." When asked by her startled audience why this should be so, she continued, "If only enough of us could get into Hell we'd soon put a stop to all that suffering. We'd convert the Devil, clean the place up, and make sure the people in it were penitent enough to enter Heaven. The Devil daren't let us in there for fear of what we'd do. There's endless numbers of us hammering away on his doors and he's too scar to let us in. He's a coward." This homely philosophy conjures the most amusing visions of a terrified Satan with sweat streaming down his furrowed face while his shoulders are jammed against the creaking gates of Hell, his slipping claws digging n all available surfaces, and the souls of all defunct Salvationists gathering their strength for another assault on the ironwork.

Every esotericist would surely agree that our principal purpose in being alive at all is to *know ourselves.* This is one reason for classifying our entire consciousness in terms of the Holy Tree of Life, then contrasting this with the Tree of Evil. By doing so, we create a sort of printed circuit for the reception and interpretation of inner intelligence from spiritual sources. In effect we are making a mental machine for translating the deep and unlimited resources of the "universal consciousness" into the limited and focal terms of our lesser human awareness. This in turn improves us as creatures of consciousness ourselves, and so the Great Work of our growing towards Godhood goes on. Of course the Tree of Life is not the only device for aiding this purpose, but it is one of the most potent and practical available anywhere.

The intention of opening ourselves inwardly to the intelligence behind the Tree is usually sufficient to at- tract attention towards ourselves, but it helps to concentrate especially upon the spheres of contact required, and here detailed knowledge and under- standing of the Tree-system is essential. This particularly includes a comprehension of its dualities and the *Middle Pillar* procedures for equilibrating its energies. Once anyone becomes familiar with the func tions and spiritual systems outlined by the Tree- design, it will respond to whoever holds its framework within their minds while aiming for an answer to problems posed.

"Messages" from this inner source rarely communicate themselves in lengthy verbalized forms. They usually come by means of "implantations" of coded consciousness which might be termed spiritual shorthand, or cosmic computerese. The recipient is then responsible for translating this into extended terms of whatever earthly language might be required. This is not unlike being given a recorded tape which in itself is only a plastic ribbon coated with magnetizable material. This has been subjected to variations of magnetic strength corresponding with original sonics. The cassette can be seen at a glance complete with knowledge of its technical nature, but to interpret its imprinted message, there has to be a special machine for converting its magnetic variants back to audible sonics, and then it may take half an hour or more to hear, let alone the much longer period to think about and consider into complete comprehension. Once all this is realized, t re should be much less anxiety about apparent non-response 0earnest inquiries.

Human interpretations of communications from "higher consciousness" can often be very wrong indeed, especially those that concern adversities in life. These should never be attributed to evil alone without good reason for absolute certainty is beyond all doubt. Adversity may equally proceed from good, or simply from natural necessity for correction by such specific means. All adversity, evil or otherwise should be treated as opportunity for identity enhancement regardless of origins. Once the type of Adversity can be classified, invocations of a appropriate spiritual agencies are a use- ful form of counter consciousness. This was once called" offering up sufferings God." In other words saying something like, "This is something more than I can bear or deal with on my own, so please beat with me. *You* find out what it feels like through me as a hum being who is part, of You. Make these sufferings Yours and th maybe they will be easier for me."

It may be noticed that when people do not experience much adversity as they need to develop themselves spiritual: they will invent or invite it on themselves imaginatively. Many of people's worries and troubles which obviously come from self-sources and are frequently termed neuroses, have been instinctively constructed quite deliberately for the specific purpose of struggling with them in hopes of benefit from the exercise. The trouble is that their creators are usually unaware of this on any objective level of consciousness, and so they build their bogies without real knowledge of their polarized needs. Therefore the outcome is frequently a bad one due to ignorance and stupidity. Their instincts were right, but their evaluations wrong.

The following chapters discuss the problem of good and evil in greater depth. Self-rulership is the greatest of all efforts earth, and is only earned by gearing good to the conversion evil. The power produced by both polarities can then be devoted to spiritual progress.

Chapter Two

The Problem of Evil

T he problem of evil has always fascinated philosophers, mystics, and spiritual speculators of every sort. Definitions and identifications of evil proliferate into confused complexities that defy satisfactory conclusions of any rational type. For some schools of thought, evil is a positive force threatening the creations and creatures of a fundamentally good God. For others, it is simply the negation of an inherently beneficent Divine Will in all life. Others again see evil as purely relative with regard to experience. There are so many valid ways of considering the same topic of evil that the only point of agreement among all is its actual existence.

This in itself is interesting. All thinking and feeling beings admit some recognition of a principle they believe is evil, no matter how they would define this in terms relative to their own consciousness and comprehension. Different individuals often designate the same factor either good or evil, depending on their variant relationships with it. The good or evil of life lies not essentially in its integrals or events, but in our own spiritual associations with all these. If we are seeking to isolate the pure principles of good and evil, we must first look inside ourselves. After that, we might start thinking about other categories of living consciousness which connect up with us via the cosmos we share with them. When we can find our own Gods and Devils that characterize us as individual entities, these will lead us to their more potent prototypes in larger areas of life altogether. There is no use whatever finding evils in others we have ignored in ourselves.

What usually attracts the attention of people to evil as a subject is its synonymity with enormous power and potential. They see evil as a main motivation behind what life is doing to them, or might enable them to practice on less powerful people. So far as they are concerned, "evil" seems to get things done which "good" disapproves of, but appears powerless to prevent. In other words, if they are the victims of some mysterious "greater evil", enough of it might rub off on them to give them a grip upon still more defenceless fellow-creatures. Most people would accept the hardest blows from life willingly enough, providing this produced in themselves a power to hit somebody else for a profit of some kind. Since this calls for expert exchanges of energy, however, few succeed very greatly along these lines, but those who do may become formidable enemies of their unhappy associates. Power-worship is probably the most facile way of proliferating evil effects among living beings.

The attraction of evil as a principle lies in its possibilities as a power-source capable of being used to pro- duce whatever its employers demand. An admittedly dangerous power-source, but nevertheless one which should theoretically prove amenable to skilfully applied safeguards. Outwitting the devil was always a major motif in magical folklore.

Perhaps there is some significance in the fact that one

kind of popular old-time magic centred round the idea of raising evil spirits to perform whatever work was demanded of them. Good spirits were only expected to see that the baddies obeyed orders. There appears to be some implication herein that only evil spirits would actually do anything required by human intentions. Good spirits were more likely to expect a far higher standard of behaviour from humans than these were willing to accept. So a sort of compromise was offered by magically minded human operatives to both good and evil spirits which the humans hoped would put much profit in their private and personal purses. The spirits did the work, the humans bagged the profit. Seemingly there were no spiritual shop stewards to prevent this exploitation of hard-working evil entities. If all the fundamentals of this set-up were transferred from the spiritual into our social fields of activity, it would produce a conventional picture of profiteering bosses misusing the misguided labouring masses. Not a nice or noble view of human motivations at all, but maybe a basic angle of observation, nevertheless.

Both would-be-goods and would-be-bads alike agree that the principle of evil is inseparable from a concept of power motivated from purposes of profit according to the directing intention. Would-be-goods acknowledge the power of evil by fear, hatred, sorrow, faith in ultimate absorption by good, or however their understanding copes with the concept. Would-be-bads grasp gleefully at the calculated risk involved for the sake of immediate advantages anticipated. Neither side deny the incalculable energy associable with the principle of evil extending throughout every force-field in which we have existence. Goodies generally believe all this energy will eventually operate only in conformity with the *initiating intention of cosmos,* or what was once called "The Will of God". Baddies would rather it did nothing of the sort, but arranged itself to suit purely personal purposes. Put another way, Goodies trust to the ultimate triumph of the true self, and Baddies hope to make all possible hay while the synthetic sun of pseudo-self still shines.

There is yet another class of consciousness to consider – what might be termed the "initiated intelligence". Individuals who have earned this classification for themselves usually prefer to treat the "good-evil" problem in a rather practical way. This basically consists of converting evilly motivated energies within their reach into pure potential power which is negated into *zoic zero,* then an equivalent amount of energy may be withdrawn from that supreme source, if required and devoted to definably good areas of their spiritual anatomy. The overall effect is an apparent conversion of evil into good by a process of neutralisation and re-polarising. This may sound simple enough when baldly asserted, but whole lifetimes can be expended without achieving the art to any significant degree. Yet until enough of mankind on this earth becomes able to neutralize and convert the evils affecting their environment, so shall our social and spiritual status suffer accordingly.

How to define the principle of evil? It is reputedly combined with the fundamental of will or intention which naturally implies some kind of "entitized awareness" or responsible form of being, not necessarily human. Absolutely pure power and energy of any kind cannot possibly be good or evil *per se.* Yet energies may be employed for purposes we recognize as being good or evil. The principle of either must therefore exist entirely in the intention of whatever intelligence may be directing those energies. Questions immediately arising are those of whose intentions, why so directed, and the various whats and hows related.

Esoteric tradition informs us that originally all energy emanated into existence from the *infinite NIL* or what we might term *zoic zero.* This energy entitized into the living spirit of cosmic consciousness or the supreme being we vaguely call "God". The original intention or will of this being was, and yet is, a state of ultimate perfection in and as Itself throughout the whole of its parts. Because of its "cosmic constitution" necessity arose for some measure of autonomy to become an inherent feature of the "life-constituents" comprising the entire entity. Other-wise "living awareness" could not exist as Itself at all. In determining Its own "divine destiny", the life-spirit automatically had to allow some degree of that very ability throughout all the lesser categories of life which constituted Its complete being. By and large, the more highly developed or evolved any type of life-unit became, the correspondingly greater degree of auto- determination or "free-will" it required. At this point the key-question comes whether any given life-unit employs its energies in the service of the life-spirit in which its own "true identity" should ultimately live, or uses these same energies for purely personal profits limited to its "pseudo-self" in mundane dimensions. That is the crux where good and evil divide from each other as separate principles involved with life as a whole. Good may fairly be defined as the intention or will to achieve identity of true self in the living spirit of cosmic creation. Evil can be contra-defined as the intention or will of remaining retarded in a state of pseudo-self for the sake of its own automatic aggrandisement.

From a purely human viewpoint it is often very difficult to distinguish the difference between effects and actions motivated by these two opposite principles. Most people do not usually go through life deliberately seeking such fine distinctions and few indeed have any conscious concepts of other than their merely mortal manifestations. General notions of good and evil are therefore mainly outcomes of subjective and instinctive appreciations usually coloured by contemporary or conventionally acceptable ideology. There may be strong disagreements about what falls into which category, but the basic recognition of "good-bad" life-possibilities alone is evidence of human evolution even at its lowest possible degree. During the ages we have spent on this earth, a majority of mankind have formed some overall concepts of goods and evils that seem to persist in our concerted opinions, and so in this work these will be taken as average standards for the two types of conscious conduct we are considering.

The "knowledge of good and evil" is presumed inherent in humanity subsequent to our material appearance as biological inhabitants of this planet, but degrees of such knowledge vary over a rather vast scale. A major difficulty lies in our usual slip-shod assumption of good or ill being presented in actual events or effects rather than the volition associated with them. No matter how bad or terrible any disaster or misfortune may be, there can be no evil in it as such, unless deliberate ill-will of some kind accompanied the happening. It is possible for life to be tragic or appalling without evil, and highly pleasurable without any good except insofar as reactions are aroused among the living individuals involved. Again and again it must be emphasized in every possible way that the pure principles of good and evil arise entirely with intention, which automatically implies the fundamentals of entity and awareness. Perhaps a simple way of appreciating this all-important point is by formulating the straightforward statement of: *Good or ill depends on* **WILL**.

The next question of course is *whose* will. That of a single human? Many humans? A non-human entity? What class of entity? Plus all the queries which relate these matters together or tie them in with our individual and collective destinies. It is obvious that the fundamental of *will* can be seen from quite a number of angles. Moreover, *will* has factors of both quality and quantity. The aggregate of individual wills combined to a single purpose may be said to equal the will of a group-entity dealing with that particular issue. In theory we should be justified in assuming the united wills of all on this earth for good to represent the degree of "God-will" active among us, and our united wills for evil to signify our "devil-degree". That is, of course, if we are prepared to personify the powers of consciousness operative through our cosmos. In practice, things are not quite so simple. The evil intentions of some may be turned to good by others, and only too frequently the best of intentions become perverted into hideous evils. To mean good is no guarantee of its appearance, but fortunately to mean evil may not materialize it. On the whole, however, the majority of mankind seldom has particular intentions of practising either good or ill. Most simply act as prompted by their main Life-drives within their environmental frameworks and let issues of good or ill determine themselves as affairs fallout. Few people exercise much will one way or the other, and so what usually happens is that most of them are prepared to let the small degree of will they possess be influenced by much more active and dominant directors of human intentions. Often such sources of intervention are other human beings, but we must not suppose those are the only agents of intention in existence. It is perfectly possible for metaphysical intelligence to influence human decisions and intentions. Depending on how we are impelled, we might consider ourselves contacted by angelic or demoniac agencies. Those old names are still effective for describing categorical types of internationalised consciousness.

One important point seems entirely clear. No matter what influences are brought to bear upon any living entity, that entity is in itself responsible for its own reactions thereto. Again responsibility is a matter of degree depending upon the evolutionary status of the entity. The more evolved we are, the greater responsibility we have. Responsibility for and to what? The Spirit of Life Itself in ourselves and all we are associated with. It is the ultimate authority to which we are alone accountable for our balance of being between good or ill issues of existence. Our interpretations of the intentions of this spirit in ourselves and otherwise are relative to our degrees of responsibility and evolvement. In the light of our past and present psycho-social history it would not seem that, as a whole, humanity has advanced very high upon the ladder of life. Nevertheless, our progress is definitely perceptible over a broad range of vision, and if it is to continue effectively we must prepare to increase our individual and collective fields of responsibility very greatly. This, of course, calls for conscious and competent control of these areas, or truly "knowing" both good and evil.

Initiated intelligence sees this problem in the following overall light. Every created entity of any description emerges from the same life-source with some specific intention in it projected from that point. This is sometimes called the "true will" inherent in us. Ultimate fulfilment of that particular will through living experience results in achievement of "true identity" or "real selfhood" in the supreme life-spirit, which could be described as a state of *perfect peace profound* because it passes our entire understanding. Thus, if we acted according to the spirit which began our being, we would live, act and evolve only as the "divine intention" within us directed, and thus develop into the perfect specimens of spiritual self we were meant to become originally.

So what went wrong with us? Nothing that cannot ultimately be righted. Having a measure of autonomy of free-will, we diverted our life-energies into incorrect channels on lower levels, and so built up artificial egoic existences which may be fairly described as states of "pseudo-self". This was our so called "fall". Inner tradition tells that man was not originally intended as a biologically breeding native of the animal kingdom at all, but that our primal progenitors' wilful infringement of procreative principles resulted in the routing of human entities through these unsatisfactory channels until we learn how to live in better states of being. That was so-called "original sin", because once human lives were bound up with physical sex-reproduction, they were automatically condemned to stay in those birth-death-rebirth cycles until they discovered methods of escape from them or bred themselves out in the course of sheer evolution.

Those of us who have become human entities involved with a destiny of doom or deliverance upon this planet are faced with only three alternatives of action:

1.　We can try directing our living in accordance with the divine intention in us so that we shall eventually evolve beyond embodied limits of being and become the better life-types of entity we were meant to be in the first place. Anything we are able to do in this direction may fairly be considered as good, leading towards central cosmic perfection.

2.　We may continue to build up our artificial egos or pseudo-selves from incarnation to incarnation on this earth from misguided motives of procuring powers or personal aggrandisements producing an illusory state of self-importance mistaken for success in living. What we do in this way cannot be other than evil.

3.　We may abandon our entitlements to entity altogether: and commit "spiritual suicide" by rejecting life at its deepest levels in us. This is the "sin against the holy spirit which cannot be forgiven", for the simple reason that there is no entity remaining to be offered other life-chances or "forgiveness". At the end of an entity all its integrals are absorbed into other aspects of life and its energies used otherwise, so nothing is actually wasted, although the original intention in that entity cannot: reach fulfilment if it ceases existing by its own will. Since this seemed like "robbing God of a Life" it was held in particular abhorrence by old-time initiates. Especially since they had reasons for believing that if any entity ended its existence intentionally, others would be called on to assume its abandoned responsibilities.

Most of us seem to steer a vacillating course between alternatives 1 and 2, with a probable preponderance of the second to minor degrees. After all, both good and evil are limited by abilities of either, and there is only so much of each that humans can possibly account for. Sufficient unto each life is the evil thereof. Besides, with such a thin line between the two principles, few can distinguish the difference until this becomes very obvious indeed. At the lower end of the life-scale there are so many enjoyable evils and so few pleasurable goods that the pseudo-self extremities of our consciousness find far more opportunities for expression via the former rather than the latter course.

It would be a mistake to suppose that our pseudo-self projections into materialized and mortal forms are evil as such. They can be lived through, experience life at this level, feedback resultant energies required by the true self, receive and transmit energies from that spiritual power-source in terms our average life-level may deal with usefully, and act as very valuable agents in our world for an *inner* authority which rightly belongs to a better state of being. Used in the right way, pseudo-self can become a sound spiritual asset. Evil arises entirely from pseudo-self seeking to establish an egoic position and authority which rightly belongs to the true self level of entity alone. To clarify this issue somewhat further, let us see it in the broadest possible light.

As life-entities, we are supposed to be creatures with a clear circulation of energy in a cosmically cyclic pattern centred on the true-self point originated by the initial intention of the life-spirit which made us what we essentially are and ought to be. The cosmic circulation of our life-energies should be centrifugally as far as our existence extends through all life-levels, then centripetally back to the perfect poise of our spiritual identity again. Providing the total energy in such a living self-cosmos were equably and properly distributed according to the constant of its creation, it would be an absolutely balanced being. Whether this ideal condition is possible on this planet or in factual practice somewhere away from our world is beside the point. It is certainly not the state of an average or even above average human at present. We are mostly very rough similitudes of that perfect spiritual pattern indeed, and it is only by knowledge of our malfunctions that we usually manage to make guesses of what we could be like if only we might get ourselves into correct cosmic order.

Our main malfunction is undoubtedly unbalance of energy due to over-emphasis of egoic concentration at the pseudo-self extremity of existence. This has comparable effects to massing weight unduly at one point of a flywheel's perimeter, or causing the electric current in a complicated circuit to rise dangerously in one area due to short-circuiting or interference with design. The overall outcome is to make the whole machinery unstable and unsatisfactory in total fulfilment of function. Because of its construction it may continue in action with perhaps many componental faults, just as our bodies will work with missing pieces and considerable organic damage. Nevertheless, neither our physical bodies nor our metaphysical make-ups can possibly operate as they were intended to if important areas have gone wrong or some vital part is failing badly. In the case of an average human the issue is usually one of simple inadequacy which can normally be compensated for otherwise until the self-structure eventually comes into a satisfactory condition. Nothing very serious that cannot be corrected over the course of time with effort. It might be said in a way that we suffer with eradicable evils as a rule. Beyond a certain limit of tolerance, however, the effects of evil increase to very dangerous proportions.

This is traceable to a single cause: Deliberate or willed isolation of egoic autonomy at the material end of the self-spectrum for the sake of establishing an apparently independent condition of entity apart from the life-spirit of cosmos itself whereto we properly belong. In old-fashioned language, Man trying to set up apart from God in a state of self-sufficiency. This is only possible to the degree anyone might live on reserve-holdings for a limited life-extent if cut off from main sources of supply. For instance, we might live without breathing for a couple of minutes, without drinking for several days, or without eating for a very few weeks. It is possible to set up a self-state at the pseudo-self end of our entire entities which is capable of simulating what seems like a whole-self-hood within its own environs. This will even extend for perhaps several incarnations before eventual break-up, because whatever separates spiritually from its natural supply of life-energy has only a limited term of existence remaining. However this term may be artificially expanded and extended, it must terminate in ultimate extinction unless reconnection to the life-source becomes possible. So we may take some long-term hope from the fact that *evil eventually extinguishes itself.* Since in human values this may take many millennia, it is scarcely a very great consolation.

The question is, of course, why any entity, human or otherwise, would want to separate away from its cosmic self-cycle of life and confine its existence into a lesser state of limitation culminating in a calculated extinction. Why accept so much less than its ultimate entitlements? Inevitably the answer is for the sake of short-term profits and pressurized powers which produce illusions of self-importance, grandeur, and other gratificatory experiences on low life-levels. We human entities have free-will *within our Self-circles,* and how we distribute our energies around them. We instinctively know our life-purpose to be the attainment of *identity as an individual.* The whole point is whether we are prepared to accept the long, difficult and demanding "cosmic climb leading steadily up the ladder of life toward our ultimate truth, or "fall for" an inferior imitation of such an achievement limited to life on this lower level.

It does not follow for one moment that all those who concern themselves with mundane matters are souls "lost to light". Far from it. We have to deal with matter on our way back to conditions of spirit, and it is incumbent on us to bring our living in this world as close to perfection as its limits allow. All this takes the time and experience of almost innumerable human incarnations. What matters is the way we bias our beings deliberately away from the spiritual end of ourselves in order to inflate an artificial ego in the opposite direction. The more energy we put into this process the greater degrees of evil we practice. Nevertheless, it takes far more energy directed with a well-developed intelligent Intention needed for either end-result. Adepts of either good or evil are relatively rare in human shape. Most of us are still amateurs, which is fortunate for us all, because even moderate experts of evil can cause enough harm among humanity as it is.

At earth-level, evil frequently seems more powerful or impressive than good. Why? The very simple reason is that for the same actual amount of pure energy expended for good or evilly motivated intentions, the effects of the latter seem greater at earth-level because it is confined within a much smaller area than the former. We might liken this to the same quantity of explosive detonated in a room full of people, or in the middle of desert with the same people scattered widely around. In the first case the energy released would probably kill them all, but in the second they might not even hear more than a feeble bang-if that. Because evil concentrates at the pseudo-self end of our entities it seems to fill up the entire field we are able to view through egoic eyes in this limited locality. Since the good we accomplish is absorbed into a far greater spiritual sell-area and normally concentrates at a point rather removed from our material foci, it may seem less real to those who live with their eyes glued to the ground. The more good we effect, the more does this limit and confine evil within lessening boundaries, which intensifies its appearance as it diminishes in actual amount. A single and sharply defined evil of a spectacular sort is most noticeable against a background of steady overall good. It is necessary to bear points like this in mind when trying to assess actualities of good or ill with an ordinary consciousness. Though the evils of this world may be only too painfully obvious, we should always consider the background of fundamental good in us which makes these ills loom so large by sheer contrast.

Now we need to be rather more specific and consider just which types of human activity can be classified as distinctly evil insofar as they debase our natures away from finer possibilities and spoil our spiritual chances of cosmic continuity towards our true ultimate identity. There must be some kind of a standard for calculating such categories of ill-doing. Here it is proposed to follow the famous *Tree-of-Life system* which is the backbone of Qabalistic and Magical inner teaching and tradition. This sets up a universal life-standard against which all that is concerned with being and becoming may be measured and estimated in relation to our best cosmic interests. Since evil forms a considerable percentage of our living behaviour, it should be calculable in terms of this remarkable Tree.

There will be no long explanations of the Tree given at this point, because so much literature is already available on that on that one topic. Some basic acquaintance with it already must be assumed, or the subject gleaned from reference works as we go along. Without at least some conceptions of what the Tree is all about, it would scarcely be possible to follow the inner trends and indications of modern Western esotericism pointing to our immediate channels of spiritual regeneration. Therefore beyond a conventional diagram of the Tree and its associated items for purposes of reference, there will be no particular recapitulation of its fundamental functions.

An immediately obvious impression of the Tree is that all its attributes, and particularly its combinational areas called "spheres" are essentially "good" or neutral in character. Not a trace of evil appears anywhere in its design. As it stands, the Tree is a design of what life should be, rather than as we must admit we find it in this world. The Tree is a plan of perfection more than a statement of fact, as we know affairs are here. The principles proclaimed by the Tree are those of our highest possible ethical standards. We see an uncompromising array of incontrovertible basics in life-behaviour which call for our finest codes of conduct if they are observed in practice. They are what might be called "cosmic commandments" which have to be followed faithfully if we ever intend becoming more than merely mortal expendables of existence. They state quite plainly and simply that if any living being intends to raise itself from humanity to a state of divinity it must cultivate and control the quality-principles of *Stability, Honour, Achievement, Harmony, Discipline, Compassion, Experience, Understanding, and Wisdom.*

Those are the points which the Tree of Life proclaims as its principles. It is quite clear that any soul able to apply all these within itself and live within a wider framework of them applied among others would arrive at very advanced cosmic conditions of life. What, on the other hand, happens in the case of those who either apply them inadequately, or else refuse to recognize them as standards, and deliberately attempt to reverse their effects?

Qabalistic tradition becomes very obscure on these issues. While reiterating again and again that no evil can possibly be permanently associated with such a holy design as the Tree of Life, allusions are made to mysterious adverse influences called in Hebrew "Klippoth", said to mean "shells, cortices, or even harlots". Whatever these may be, very few references have much to say about them in explicit terms. It is almost as if a tacit agreement existed among exponents of Qabalah that if these unpleasant issues were ignored they might eventually disappear altogether under some convenient cosmic carpet. Such a policy may have seemed admirable to bygone authorship, but since then experience of world events has rather led us into dragging our demons out into the light of clear understanding where they will wither away as they deserve. If evil is our worst enemy, then it may only be overcome by our knowledge of its workings and capabilities. Let us see, therefore, what we can discover about these *Klippoth* which seem to lurk in the shadows of our *Life-Trees* to poison their fruits and ultimately cut off their roots from that spiritual garden in which they originated.

The word "Klippoth" does not tell us very much as it stands, being ambiguous and uncertain in meaning. Its roots, however, are much more informative:

QLL: to vilify, curse, or to bring a curse on oneself.

QLQL: mean and vile.

PVTh: to be apart or separated.

PTh: interstice, or a space between things.

PThVTh: euphemism for the female pudenda, or "hinge", signifying the sockets that receive the phallic hinge-pin of the door.

With these few meanings quite a number of important ideas appear at once. We get an immediate impression of an unhappy life-state due to having brought accursed conditions on ourselves by separation from something or someone. In some way we have prostituted ourselves and become empty vessels (shells) like hollow sockets from which the pin has been withdrawn. Rather a clever Qabalistic opinion of evil. A curse we bring on ourselves by trying to separate away from divine goodness, which, if withdrawn from us leaves us empty as an open socket. Quite a fair commentary for a few terse root-meanings. Evil is shown here as a lessening and worsening of ourselves. There is not the least suggestion that a practice of evil might make us into powerful and mighty malignant masters of anything at all. On the contrary, a state of spiritual stupidity and general sadness is implied. Perhaps the *Klippoth* might be defined as the vilifiers of the *Tree-Principles,* who intend to separate from these, and prevent them from coming to fruition if possible.

Exorcising the Tree of Evil

Table 2.1. Oppositions to the Tree of Life

Tree of Life		Tree of Evil
The Kingdom (of God).	10	*.Materialism*
Foundation (of Life)	9	*Instability*
Glory.	8	*Greed*
Achievement .	7	*Lust*
Beauty (Harmony)	6	*Inharmony*
Discipline	5	*Cruelty*
Compassion	4	*.Apathy*
Here the Abyss is crossed by Experience.		Here the Abyss is imposed by Ignorance
Understanding	3	*Antipathy*
Wisdom.	2	*Stupidity*
The.Apex.of.Spirit	1	*Atheism*
Light.	0	*Darkness*

Maybe the childish term "baddies" suits them best.

To classify the *Klippoth* (which is a plural word, the singular being "Klippah") we need only look for the diametrically opposite quality, or lack of quality, in the case of each sphere or item on the Tree of Life. Table 2.1 will give us a sound overall idea of what the "opposition", or "Satan the Adversary" amounts to as a set of concepts preventing the perfection of humanity. When we see this as a picture which may be contrasted against the true Tree of Life glyph, it makes a very interesting presentation. Take the straightforward check-list for instance, from the bottom upwards.

A rather horrifying contrast, but those opposing factors are to be found readily enough in our world and we cannot evade or escape them by pretending otherwise. There is at least one hopeful indication. Being directly related with each other as oppositionals, it must therefore be possible to transmute or convert the lesser factors into fractions of the greater, or "overcome evil with good". Possible, but certainly not an easy problem to solve in practice. Theoretically the same life-energy that we divert into evilly intentioned channels of action could perfectly well be put to good uses by altering the polarity of our inner intentions. All the evil we work in this world might be converted into good if only the aggregate of our combined *wills* switched to the other side of *self,* so to speak. Cynicism apart, owing to the unlikelihood of such an event in the foreseeable future, the possibility and principles of this must be accepted. Even though we are not prepared to hope the majority of mankind would ever allow an alteration in actuality, it may yet prove practical for individuals to attempt. Therefore we shall be justified in pushing our inquiries as far as we can along these lines.

The side pillars and central support of the Tree of Evil are interesting.They consist of the extremities of *compulsion* on one side, *coercion* on the other, and *condemnation* in the middle. In the case of the Tree of Life, these are respectively *severity, mildness,* and *moderation.* This is to indicate that we should always look for a middle course of life between extremities of hardness on one side or softness on the other. A central ideal ought always to be looked for in every event of life, and the design of the Tree tells us this quite plainly. The Tree of Evil sets a middle course of *condemnation* between extremities of *compulsion* and *coercion.* We curse or damn ourselves to the extent we deliberately apply coercive or compulsive means of driving ourselves or others into evil courses. Both of these drives imply intentional interference with a will or wills which might otherwise have inclined toward good. It is implied with the factors of compulsion and coercion that they are only employed in the service of evil intentions. People cannot be either compelled or coerced into doing good. They may be induced by such means into conformity with dictates and that is all.

No wonder we are such difficult creatures to deal with. There is such a narrow difference between our opting for good or ill that most of the time we seldom stop to bother which course we are pursuing. Intelligence and reason do not decide the issue, they simply exploit or direct it. We cannot develop the qualities of the Tree in ourselves by any amount of training or education. They are natural fundamentals of our living which come from the depth of our Inner characters. For good or ill we make ourselves with them as souls and potentially immortal entities. They are the distinctive categories of conscious energy out of which we have to construct what amounts to our cosmic identities, or else eliminate ourselves out of existence by working the wrong way with the life-forces which keep us in being. The qualities of the life-tree *are* the characteristic energies which enable us to exist at all. Without them we just should not be alive in any condition whatever. It is as well to remember that point. Used one way the energies will enhance and expand our living beyond any mortally embodied restrictions imposed by materialized life on this or other planets. Used (or misused) in an opposite manner, the same energies will only expand the limited living of our separative pseudo-selves until these explode or expire, unless they contrive artificial extension of their conditions by what amounts to real black magic. Even this "borrowed", or rather *stolen,* state of imitation selfhood must necessarily be doomed to ultimation extinction. No one can cheat the laws of cosmic life for ever.

Our main concern in contrasting the Tree of Life with the Tree of Evil should therefore be to discover how we can hold our living energies in the pattern of the first, and prevent their degeneration into the adverse activities of the second. Additionally we need to know how we may tackle the energies we engender or encounter in the course of evil so that these will neutralize and convert into their complementary counterparts on the living tree. Such ought to be the objectives of our metaphysical exercise. We may as well start by examining the oppositional pairs in their order, and looking for common denominators to serve for conversion point.

Chapter Three

Making Both Ends Meet

It is often assumed that our good and evil activities are quite apart from each other and have nothing in common. This is completely fallacious. Human activity as such is limited within a definite range of capabilities and good or ill motivations can extend through them all. An action is an action which means expenditure of energy, and energy *per se* is always convertible into other terms. For example, a person or persons may intend evil and act accordingly. The energies involved may be contained within a greater field which is controlled by those intending good and so, in the long run, will good be made of evil. The same has to be true in the case of evil. If well-meaning but weak people act with good intentions but feeble effect, this may be commandeered by intelligent agents of evil motives, and misappropriated accordingly. These are indeed the "good intentions; that pave the way to hell". They did so because they were feeble and foolish in the first place. Were it not for even greater intelligences acting in the interests of cosmic intentions, we should be on much lower life-levels than we are.

Why do we not see this clearly enough? Largely because from a purely human viewpoint the effects of applied evil are usually so perceptible in terms of

Table 3.1   SPHERE 10

Tree of Life *The Kingdom (of God)*		Tree of Evil *Materialism*
I am here to experience Life	1	Life is here for me to experience.
Everything matters.	2	Matter is everything.
Evolve through animal life.	3	I live as an evolved animal
I will become myself only in the One Life of Spirit.	4	I will have only this one Earth life to become myself.
I can get all I ought	5	I ought to get all I can.
It is impossible to exist without Spirit	6	The existence of Spirit is Impossible.
I will relate all Life by its common denominator of the Living Cosmic spirit. Controlled by that in me I shall become what I will in it.	7	I will relate all on Earth by the common denominator of money. As I control that, so shall I do what I want in this world
I cannot live on Earth without a body.	8	Without an earthly body I cannot live.
I can believe in anything not excepting this physical world	9	I cannot believe in anything excepting this physical world.
Eat and drink so that if we die tomorrow we shall be merry	10	Eat, drink, and be merry, for tomorrow die.

time-space-effects, and the greater area of good which contains these, seems relatively distant and beyond immediate importance. It is also true that those who are closely wrapped up in immediate short-term illusory apparent benefits usually fail to notice the confines of arranged evil round the pseudo-self, put there for "soul-bait". This is why we are told so often not to fight evil with evil, but to "overcome evil with good", or grow to such spiritual stature that we are capable of containing, neutralizing and converting ill-intentioned energies with an ever-increasing degree of ability.

Let us take a look at this problem in practical appearance on the Tree of Life as contrasted against the "Tree of

Evil". It can scarcely be emphasized enough that the Tree of Life cannot be perverted or made to symbolize evil *per se*. The Tree of Evil is only an outline of what would be produced if the qualities of the life-tree were deliberately and intentionally rejected in favour of their diametrical opposites. It is a theoretical presentation what ought *not to be lived* so that the Tree of Life may truly prosper in the souls and spirits of those seeking its cultivation. In effect it is as if anyone said, "If I am to be disciplined I must not be cruel; if I mean to be merciful I must not be apathetic; if I will to be wise, then I must not be stupid", and so forth. The Tree of Evil is simply to tell us what has to be negated in order to recover the equivalent energies in the appropriate category of the Tree of Life. It is quite true that the energies of good qualities may be reversed into evil courses intentionally. The risk and responsibility for this must be incurred and accepted by whoever is deranged or depraved enough to intend it. For such, the Tree of Evil can provide nothing more than a passport to ultimate perdition. For those intending their own self-salvation, the Tree of Evil offers a valuable set of instructions in activity avoidance and a table of energy-conversion which can be of the greatest spiritual service. So we shall make use of it at present.

Suppose we take a few factors applying to Stage 10 on the Trees, and see what the linkage is. In this case we shall have to note the connections between a soul struggling on the Tree of Life to recognize the rulership of *divinity* in this material world, and another soul purely concerned in the same sphere on the Tree of Evil with becoming the biggest pseudo-self here that it can. Each being would see the same integers arranged differently for opposite purposes. A set of these ideas is shown in Table

Table 3.2   SPHERE 9

Tree of Life Foundation		Tree of Evil Instability
What matters in Life is that all should have a chance.	1	Life is all a matter of chance.
Live in stability.	2	Live in instability.
Be responsible in living.	3	Live irresponsibly in being.
Place faith in no "thing"	4	Place faith in nothing.
The meaning of Life is found in Infinite Nil.	5	There is no meaning to be found in Life.
Growth under control.	6	Grow uncontrollably.
Be discriminate in breeding.	7	Breed indiscriminately.
The significance of society is in families.	8	Families are socially insignificant.
Sex is of some importance to all.	9	Sex is something all important.
Life is certainly All.	10	All Life is uncertain.

3.1.

Ten ways of dealing with life on the bottom sphere of its tree. In each case the same fundamental notions are angled in different directions to produce opposing viewpoints. One polarity shows life as being entirely confined to physical levels applying to humans for one incarnation only, during which they should get all they can out of it. The other end of the same scheme reveals an evolving entity progressing through and past material living towards a spiritual status independent of earth-existence.

Everything depends on how we polarize our self-circuits, and this in turn depends upon our individual wills. Perhaps a cynic might say our lack of will. It is true that average humans vacillate with only small degrees of will between both extremities, but this does not alter the fact that they could dedicate themselves either way if they so choose. Eventually, they might even learn the "middle method" of progression towards a state of spiritual life-perfection termed simply *peace profound* because it passes our understanding entirely.

Instead of stopping to analyse each point carefully here let us go straight on to the next sphere of the tree. This is classified as "foundation", and deals with basics of life which should give us stability, such as our families, our faiths, aims, and so forth. It also concerns fertility of body, mind, and soul, insofar as it provides the equivalents of genes out of which we have to build up our own life-entities. Looked at from similar standpoints on both Trees of Life and Evil, we might select another contracting ten ideas as shown in Table 3.2.

Another ten inversals taking place through the same sphere of the tree. It might be necessary to remind ourselves here that the nil-factor is taken mystically to mean the ultimate *zoic zero* or point at which we pass beyond being human altogether. Therefore it is the highest possible *positive* aim of every initiated individual. It is only when people begin to appreciate the incredible potential of what others consider "nothing" that they commence the reversal of their polarities which results in living "upwardly and inwardly" towards infinite light. In fact, it is exactly this change of polarity away from pseudo-self and back towards the true self which marks an initiated soul from one which has not yet begun this process of its own free will. To initiate means to begin, and once we have commenced our changed course of inner cosmos in conformity with what amounts to our true wills, then we may be classified as genuine initiates of Life.

Table 3.3.   SPHERE 8

| Tree of Life | | Tree of Evil |
Glory (Honour)		Greed
You cannot cheat Life without paying.	1	You cannot make Life pay without cheating.
Know the import of being a Self.	2	Be known by your self-importance
Take every advantage to benefit others for your own good.	3	Take every advantage of others for your own benefit.
Be not deceived.	4	To deceive is nothing.
Don't steal it – earn it.	5	Don't earn it – steal it.
It is foolish to enjoy flattery.	6	Enjoy the flattery of fools
Grasp what being means.	7	Be mean and grasping.
Be clever, make others think.	8	Make others think you're clever.
Admire the possibilities of learning.	9	Learn how it is possible to be admired.
Laugh with others at what happens	10	Laugh at what happens with others.

No synthetic lodge or temple titles will ever confer this degree upon us. It is something we must earn of our own accord entirely. There is no other way.

To continue with our tree-contrasts, we shall branch out to the next sphere of *glory* or *honour*. This is concerned with the principles of life which provide incentives for us to develop ourselves in fair and legitimate ways which will bring credit to us, yet harm no one. Its opposite number in terms of evil is just plain *greed* which cares nothing for how much anyone else may be hurt as long as objectives are gained by hook or by crook. A set of contrasts may read like Table 3.3

Looking at the "evil" side of this tree we can see a rather unpleasant sort of person sneering back, but who would

Table 3.4   *SPHERE 7*

Tree of Life Victory (Achievement)		Tree of evil Lust
Overcome Evil with Good	1	Overcome Good with Evil
Achieve what is Right	2	Achievement is your right
Be master of your Self	3	Be the master yourself
Desire to be satisfied.	4	Satisfy your desires
Make your forces obey your will	5	Make your will obeyed by force.
Be it against your will to use compulsion on others.	6	Use your compulsion on others against their will.
Let no cost be unaccounted for.	7	Count not any costs.
Break nothing you cannot make.	8	Break to nothing what you cannot make.
Conquer hate.	9	Hate and conquer.
Oppose all intending to destroy you.	10	Destroy all intending to oppose you.

be rash enough to deny some slight reflections of his own inner appearance? There should be little doubt, however, about where the dividing line between the two polarities comes. If we cross over the tree-plan to the next sphere altogether, it may seem similar to the last because it is called *victory* on the good side and plain *lust* on the bad. *Lust* and *greed* are not exactly the same at all. *Greed* indicates some degrees of cunning and even perverted intelligence, but *lust* signifies a "get it at all costs" outlook. Lust will even destroy itself in achieving an objective, or destroy the objective to prevent anyone else achieving it. Greed may be temporarily satiated, but lust is unquenchable. Where greed would infiltrate, lust must dominate. Its "victory" is so often purely pyrrhic. A contrasting tree at this sphere could read like table 3.4

A concentration of the Tree of Evil characteristics on this sphere would certainly produce a dangerous and vi-

Table 3.5   *SPHERE 6*

Tree of Life		Tree of Evil
Beauty (Harmony)		Ugliness (Discord)
Control chaos, then create what you will.	1	Create chaos, then control what you will.
In a universe of Eternal Beauty, all ugliness must face away.	2	In Universal Ugliness, Beauty must fade away forever.
Whoso rules out Beauty blasts the world.	3	Whoso blasts out Beauty rules the world.
Discover what prevents people from knowing the difference between Beauty and Ugliness.	4	Prevent people from discovering the difference between Beauty and Ugliness.
Truth strikes up in Harmony.	5	Inharmony strikes out at Truth.
Never persuade people to accept ugliness.	6	Persuade people to accept Ugliness or nothing.
Keep in control of yourself.	7	Keep yourself in control.
Control confusion in yourself and others.	8	Confuse others, then control them yourself.
Make opportunities for others to regain lost balance	9	Unbalance others to make opportunities for yourself.
The secret of perfection lies in preventing deliberate disorganization	10	In deliberate disorganization lies the secret of preventing perfection.

cious person. Yet the same factors turned round could result in a very noble and potent being. The next sphere ought to show up some interesting contrasts too because it is that of *beauty,* or *harmonious balance.* If this is not perfectly true to its centre, then the poise of the entire plan is bound to be affected Glancing from one tree to the other, we might see something like Table 3.5

Here we get a picture of an evilly intentioned being with sufficient intelligence to know quite well how to upset the processes of cosmos in his own self-circles for very anti-cosmic motives. It is natural that the higher we climb the tree the more advanced we shall find the degree of

Table 3.6   *SPHERE 5*

Tree of Life Severity (Discipline)		Tree of Evil Cruelty
Be strictly just.	1	Just be strict.
Hate to hurt.	2	Hurt and hate.
Conquer the will to kill.	3	Will to kill or conquer.
Feel for ill treatment of others.	4	Ill-treat the feelings of others.
Revenge is wrong.	5	Revenge all wrongs.
Be severe only in necessity.	6	It is necessary to be severe.
Respect whose will not punish you.	7	Punish whoso will not respect you.
Be fearful of ever being brutal.	8	Be brutal, and feared forever.
Force ferocity to be subdued.	9	Subdue by ferocious force.
Discipline yourself to make others accept you.	10	Make others accept your discipline

adepthood either way. An interesting point here is that evil entities show recognition of their own limitations. They realize they could not entirely destroy the workings of cosmos at this particular point without breaking up their own pseudo-selves also. Therefore they learn how to create a controllable chaos which affects others adversely yet leaves their own main interests clear. Such as outbreaks of civil violence, contained warfare, inexplicably altered economies, and carefully directed con- fusions of thinking coupled with attacks on basic beliefs. If asked for their own beliefs, they might reply cynically that the hand which rocks human concepts of order and balanced beliefs may also rule this world. It is all a question of tipping the balance of everything toward their own favour.

The next sphere up the tree is a really stringent one. In *good* terms it signifies *discipline*, economy, strict justice,

Table 3.7   *SPHERE 4*

| Tree of Life | | Tree of Evil |
Mercy (Compassion)		Apathy (Indifference)
Nothing is too much trouble for anything.	1	Everything is too much trouble for nothing.
Don't let anything bother you.	2	Don't be bothered with anything.
Care for others that have none to care.	3	Care not for the cares of others.
Be merciful. Waste no time.	4	Waste no time being merciful.
Where there is generosity there is no necessity.	5	There is no necessity for generosity.
Have compassion on the weak.	6	It is weak to have compassion.
Life should be too happy for weariness.	7	Life is too wearing for happiness.
Live, love, and laugh.	8	It is laughable to try loving life.
Answer anyone in need.	9	Needless to answer anyone.
Make efforts to help anyone worthwhile.	10	Is it worthwhile making efforts to help anyone?

and all the qualities of correct training at any life-level. On the *evil* side it degenerates into plain and horrible *cruelty*. Again the factors are convertible. We can change to either side at will. Table 3.6 shows how one set of contrasts could read.

This gives a decided impression of someone who could be vicious and vengeful on one side, or a disciplined devotee to duty on the other. Again and again these contrasting trees keep reminding us of the saying, "The greater the sinner the greater the saint". It is amazing sometimes what a thin hairbreadth separates one state from the other. Take the next sphere, for instance. On the good side, we have a magnanimous, kindly, generous, *merciful,* and *compassionate* nature. On the other side, *indifferent,* lazy, bored, and couldn't-care-less sort of outlook which just lets life go to hell in its own hand-basket. Table 3.7 shows what a contrasting set of concepts might postulate.

Rather a concise run-down on how one person would take a set of factors and be magnanimously merciful, while another would use the same set for becoming idly irresponsible and indifferent. As always, everything turns upon the pivot of individual inclination.

We now come up against what we might as well call the "ignorance gap" in our tree-scheme. By ignorance is meant a deliberate refusal to cross the borderline between real understanding wisdom linked with acceptance of an ultimate awareness, and a state of stupid and strenuous denial that a "cosmic constant" of spiritually living consciousness exists. Ignorance implies intentional rejection of the life-spirit as a controlling consciousness of cosmos. Refusal to accept or be associated with any "divine directions" connected with our more advanced stages of conscious living. Mere lack of wisdom or under- standing *per se* is not necessarily ignorance, but may well be sheer innocence. Ignorance is always intentional, while innocence is conditional. So this is where we have to balance these two alternatives in ourselves and at least come to a personal poising point between them.

If we manage to cross the abyss which divides most of our more ordinary faculties from our highest principles of understanding and wisdom, we shall find that we have a choice even on this level of promoting or perverting the powers of either. Let us look at Table 3.8 to see how the next sphere of understanding, which naturally signifies also sympathy and intuition, could be twisted

Table 3.8   SPHERE 3

Tree of Life Understanding (Intuition)		Tree of Evil Antipathy
It is pathetic being anti-anything.	1	Be antipathetic to everything.
Understand, then you need not fear.	2	Fear what you do not understand.
Try to understand things.	3	Understanding things is trying.
Be sympathetic to the stupid.	4	Sympathy is stupid.
Understanding avoids hate.	5	Hate avoids understanding.
Don't reject anything. Listen and learn.	6	Don't listen to anything. Reject Learning
Shun dangers by intuition.	7	Intuition is dangerous, shun it.
Do no dislike what you do not understand.	8	Refuse to understand what you dislike
Who understands enough to care?	9	Who cares enough to be understood?
Comprehension passes all.	10	It is all past comprehension.

into a wilful or vindictive travesty of what it should lead us toward in life.

Level with understanding on the other side of the tree is wisdom, considered as the "masculine" complement of consciousness. This does not in the least mean that wisdom is exclusively a male prerogative. Polarity on the tree is not sexual in an ordinary sense at all, and the distinctions are simply used as convenient labels to indicate the out given or intaken complements of any complete cycle of consciousness. Here, we are dealing with the former, or outgoing type of comprehension, as distinct from the latter intuitive kind. We can contrast wisdom and stupidity as shown in Table 3.9. On the next page.

Table 3.9   *SPHERE 2*

Tree of Life Wisdom		Tree of Evil Stupidity
Where ignorance is folly it is bliss being wise.	1	Where ignorance is bliss 'tis folly to be wise.
Accept wisdom. Why be stupid?	2	Why be wise when stupidity is acceptable?
The fear of God begins wisdom.	3	Who fears the wisdom of any God?
Wisdom clarifies obscurity.	4	Obscure the clarity of wisdom.
Why play the fool when it is pleasing to work with wisdom?	5	Why work at wisdom when foolishness gives pleasure?
Among the wise, it is idiotic being stupid.	6	Among idiots the stupid seem wise.
Find out how you might encourage wisdom in others.	7	Don't encourage wisdom in others – they might find you out.
Time is never wasted with wisdom.	8	Never waste time with wisdom.
What can we do without wisdom?	9	We can do without wisdom.
Wisdom cannot afford luxuries.	10	Better luxuriously stupid than penurious wise.

Here we may see *stupidity* defined as a positive refusal to become wise for a number of what seem inadequate reasons. Yet millions of human beings utterly refuse to enlighten themselves in any spiritual way whatever for many personal motives. Very frequently the chief cause is sheer inertia, or what used to be called in good old-fashioned terms "downright laziness". Unwillingness to exert efforts except in pursuit of immediate and obvious profits. True wisdom has its sphere next to the top of the tree, and relatively few people care to climb so high in search of clearer consciousness. Most would rather stay in what seems like the safety of stupidity with the rest of the crowd. At the altitude of the *wisdom-sphere,* human

Table 3.10   SPHERE 1

Tree of Life The Crown		Tree of Evil Atheism
God is living, not dead.	1	God is dead, not living.
O God! Do what Thou wilt.	2	No God. Do what you will.
God is everywhere.	3	Wherever is God?
God is no "thing".	4	God is nothing.
Nothing is impossible with God.	5	God is nothing but impossible.
God knows who exists.	6	Who knows God exists?
Can anyone prove there is no God?	7	No one can prove there is a God.
Not everyone knows God exists.	8	Everyone knows God does not exist.
God is what anyone can place faith in.	9	What faith can anyone place in God?
Believe in God. Do not doubt Divinity	10	Don't believe in God. Doubt Divinity.

inhabitants are noticeably scarce compared with lower levels. The sharp clarified atmosphere so commonly proves too uncomfortable for those who prefer darker and damper conditions elsewhere.

Now we come right to the top of the tree and the vital issue of life itself. How are we to relate ourselves with the conscious cause of living, or the supreme spirit which mankind calls "God" by so many different titles? Do we adopt some definite attitude of awareness toward this state of being which will affect all our life-activities and consequently our ultimately self becoming? On the other hand, shall we strenuously deny the very existence or likelihood of any such "overbeing", and try to live without reference to *it* or *that* at all?

Whichever we do, it is certain that we cannot affect such a being by our attitudes, but only our own lives and what we shall become. We, and we alone, stand to gain or lose by the decisions we make at this apical point of the tree called the "crown" because it is the summit of life from which we either pass into *perfect peace* beyond, or plunge down to the depths again in search of more living experience. A contrast between the two trees might well appear as shown in Table 3.10.

This supreme issue here makes all the difference between whether we steer the whole course of our lives towards spiritual or utterly egotistical ends. The whole. issue divides upon whether or not we relate ourselves intentionally with whatever consciousness is the underlying cause of cosmos, however we term or identify this principle. Our affirmations of it will not enlarge, nor our denials of it diminish the existence of this entity by one iota. What our attitudes of awareness will accomplish are changes of our conscious relationship with all that lives, and consequently our own characters and ultimate becomings. That surely matters to everyone.

Whether we personalize the power some call "God" into intimately appreciated conditions of being, or prefer to consider It or That as an indefinitely distant and aloof influence on our affairs, is a matter for individual adjustment. The intelligent mystic normally seeks a way between both near and far extremities, focussing at median point on the middle pillar which combines either viewpoint into a satisfactory and workable concept. What matters is the actual concentration of conscious energy, and how we formalize or arrange this is usually dependent on prevailing circumstances of consciousness and availability of inner information. We make images and ideas with whatever we happen to have handy in ourselves at the time, and so these are changeable and improvable constructions. Therefore we should realize our God-images are not fixed but flexible and adaptable arrangements. Those can be altered to suit needs and contingencies. Our pure abstract "imageless" concept of ultimate entity, however, is a permanent inner area kept

deliberately clear of all else so that the divinity we dedicate this "selfspace" to may impress into us *what it wills.* Thus if we balance out the difference between both fixed and mutable angles of inner approach to supreme spirit,

we shall arrive at a reliable "cardinal" bearing by which to steer our life-course safely into a sound spiritual harbour.

Now we have covered the tree from one end to the other with a hundred convertible ideas which incline us to evil one way, good the other, or offer a chance of poise between the two principles if we are able to learn how to walk this "way of the wise". Legend says that we have

fallen to our present low evolutionary position because we demanded a free choice between good or evil. Our violent swings from one side to the other do not seem to have helped us up the Tree of Life very far as yet. Maybe

if we concentrated on keeping a clear way equidistantly from either, and progressed at a pace consistent with the constant of cosmos we should at last learn how to live in the real sense of the word. Let us see what may be done

in this vital direction.

Chapter Four

Right, Left and Centre

There are only three life-possibilities to cover the whole range of our cosmic and conscious existence. We may think of these under a wide number of headings such as:

Positive	Neutral	Negative
Yes	Maybe	No
Good	Indifferent	Bad
Plus	Equal	Minus
This	The other	That
White	Grey	Black

or any other way we like. Those are the alternatives of action which govern all we do and whatever happens to us in any condition of consciousness. They are the *three pillars* which support the Tree of Life wherever it grows, which is to say in every living soul.

With such alternatives we have again three alternative courses in their application: 1) we can simply let them all happen to and with ourselves; 2) we can deliberately make them happen of our own accord; 3) we can make a "middle mixture" of these and live accordingly.

Obviously this last is the most practical means of making sound spiritual progress, so we shall seek out methods of adjusting our lives therewith. The major method it is proposed to put forward here involves the use of what some would call "psycho-dramatic action", and others by the older description of ritual magic.

Why so? What is so special about ritualistic procedure that it might prove adequate for such a profound purpose? First and foremost it involves intentional patterns of consciousness which may be reproduced and enhanced as an when required to meet contingencies. This means a lot of other concomitants. The discipline and training of will, concentration of consciousness into con- trolled channels of purpose, interaction of inner energies between human and other types of intelligence, and many more important considerations connected with what might be termed the "metaphysical mechanics" of living. Nobody can work even minor magical rites with- out automatically employing many of these factors to some degree, even if such a degree may be very small indeed. The efficacy of any ritualism depends upon the direction of its related inner energy, and this depends again on the energy available, skill of operators concerned, pattern of "circuitry" used, and of course, capabilities and scope of the "inward and invisible" agencies of intelligence co-operating.

It takes two sorts of entity to work what may be called *magic* with any effect from an earthly basis. Embodied humans intentionally employing specific formulae of consciousness and behaviour, partnered by non-physical types of entity capable of linking in and at least generally guiding the appropriate inner energies necessary for accomplishing whatever the overall purpose of the whole operation may be. Our cosmos being constructed as it is, the actualities of this entire process are attenuated through a very deep range of reactions, and humans attempting to work it from merely "wish-want" motives are likely to be extremely disappointed by the non-results obtained. Unless, of course, they are so determined on gaining their immediate ends that they are prepared to sacrifice very valuable sections of their spiritual structures in exchange. Assuming such insanity is outside our present picture, we can take quite a practical view of the problems posed.

On one hand we see humans determined on following courses of consciousness and intention which lie rather beyond their normal powers of performance. Therefore, they decide to use so-called magical means of summative symbolism in terms of awareness and behaviour which expresses their purpose as a formula of faith and work of will. On the other hand, we may see, suppose, or otherwise postulate beings who live beyond embodiment as we know this term, well able to employ energy entirely without physical mechanisms, yet quite cognitive of patterned consciousness arranged by people living on this or other planets. A working partnership between these distinct life-levels is perfectly possible among those capable and willing to form such relationships of spiritual symbiosis.

Let us take rather an odd analogy to illustrate the situation. Suppose someone is standing on the edge of a fish-pond observing those very different life-forms going about their normal business in an element and circumstances quite incompatible with human living. If the fish are aware of the human at all, it can only be in the vaguest way, which cannot comprehend our natures or modes of living to more than the very least degree imaginable. The human watches the fish swimming around and gets a general notion of their behaviour patterns and adaptations with their circumstances. Now let us suppose a virtually incredible happening. One solitary fish starts swimming in repetitive and most peculiar patterns which turn out to be message in plain English: "H.E.L.P. M.E.". Again and again the creature spells these unmistakable words in our language. If this happened in actuality, one would hope an interested observer would summon all the aid he could in the way of veterinary and scientific specialists all motivated by a united aim of helping a fellow creature in totally different dimensions of living, yet capable of communication with us in mutually recognisable evidence of awareness.

To quite an extent, this is more or less what happens in ritual magical procedures. By carrying them out on our levels, we make symbolic signs which convey sensible communications to observers and sympathetic types of entity operating along what could be called contiguous channels of consciousness in different dimensions of living. The patterns of ordinary human living at earth-level are familiar enough to those "inner intelligences". Our behaviour to them is much what the behaviour of animals and other creatures are to us. Predictable and reasonably certain pat- terns of conditioned consciousness. Even our most insane and outrageous activities are easily calculated into anticipated cycles. In fact, the behaviour of insane humans is much more computable than that of the most balanced beings. As a species of living creature, man is a very guessable proposition to those even a little more advanced in evolution.

What happens in the case of those exceptional humans

who go beyond standards of average behaviour and aware- ness enough to make recognizable signals in terms of an "inner language" immediately intelligible by those whose common consciousness deals with similar symbology? Whatever their reactions may be, it is certain their attention will be attracted and interests aroused. Whether or not this may lead to closer relationships developing is a matter for specific settlement among those concerned. All we may be sure of at our end of earth-living is that certain formulae of consciousness and associated behaviour which some call magical are bound to make some kind of contact with other types of consciousness than ours on ordinary mortal levels among the rest of mankind. What eventuates from such an inner linkage with different orders of living intelligence than ours, depends on many factors outside our immediate control. Whether indeed this may be to our ultimate benefit or otherwise is another issue entirely. What should concern us at present is the possibility of this matter *per se*.

Applying the three points of the tree-pillars to this problem, we shall find that such extra-mundane agencies either a) exist; b) do not exist; or c) ambivalate. This means to say that the postulate of existence or non- existence apply purely to our conceptions of those limits. What has no existence for us may well be definable by an awareness operating far beyond our greatest range of experience. We are in no position to state dogmatically: "Nothing exists after such and such a point". We may quite fairly say: "I cannot conceive the existence of so and so". That would be true because it is an admission of human limitations. The central position adopted by anyone of initiated intelligence is to agree that past our furthest point of perception, where non-existence begins for most mortals, the possibility of indefinite extensions into very different dimensions must be at least accepted hypothetically. Once this balance of belief becomes workable, it then proves possible to think, act, or behave relatively to the terms of the hypothesis for the sake of experience within its operative field. Thus it is quite practical to take a midway stance between the being or unbeing of what were once called simply "spirits" but have since been promoted to becoming "paraphysical entitisations"!

Be it noted that we do not have to believe or disbelieve in the actuality of such inner agencies *per se*. What we must believe in is the possibility they exist in their own state of being, yet are capable of interaction with ours by unspecified means or degrees. In other words, we must be prepared to accept a working hypothesis and go on from there within its term of reference. We might say in effect: "Acting on the assumption that the position is such and such, I behave, think, or conduct myself accordingly". That is a perfectly legitimate standpoint for those seeking the "middle way" of magical practice. The act of faith involved does not rest in whatever inner beings may or may not be concerned, but in one's own ability to make relationships with relative metaphysical equivalents. This makes an important difference in concept. We need not believe in "spirit" unless we want to, but we positively must believe in our capability of living and behaving as if the energies available to such entities might be employed on our behalf. In some way this is rather like the personal credo of an agnostic who says firmly: "Even if there isn't a God, I shall still live as if there were one, because I honestly believe that is the best thing to do"". Here the two extremities of belief and unbelief both support the central course of conduct. This could be paraphrased by a thoughtful exponent of magic to read: "Even if magic may not work, I shall act as if it did, and then it might". Here again belief is centred in an individual's estimation of its own abilities.

It is really extraordinary how relatively little faith is needed to form a basis of magical action. Especially when nowadays people are willing to believe so much more unlikely propositions. They will readily pay for lottery tickets in the belief of becoming rich against fantastic odds. They accept the most preposterous "come-ons", the wildest and wiliest catches of advertiser and confidence tricksters. Some are even gullible enough to trust politicians' promises. There seems no end to the credulity of mankind in pursuit of phantom profits. Humans will literally believe in almost anything that activates their dual greed-fear life drives. If they ever learned how to equate these out into a centrally poised power or purpose, their faith would change direction quite dramatically. Once the force of faith shifts away from material into metaphysical channels, life itself alters into far greater areas of possibility and promise. The basics of magical beliefs are simply that energy *per se* extends indefinitely beyond physical limits, that intelligent living consciousness also exists in far finer or "spiritual" forms than are commonly known to humanity, and furthermore that relationship is possible between humans and such supraphysical extensions of energy and entity. 'Those are the bare essentials. All the rest is a matter of arrangements.

The first basic is virtually unavoidable by any rational modern mind. We are constantly faced with energy extending into dimensions of existence utterly beyond the grasp of even our immediate ancestors. Moreover, it is realized that this greatly increased range of action only covers the virtual fringe of incredibly vast areas which will eventually become accessible to our descendants. Energy as such is endless, infinite, and certainly extends beyond the extremities of our broadest and highest concepts. It needs little faith to accept this today when we live so close to its factuality.

The second basic does depend on our definitions of conscious intelligence. If we refuse to postulate this outside of merely human limits, then, of course, not only magic, but all other spheres of spiritual activity become automatically closed and non-existent to us. It also requires us to believe implicitly that conscious intelligence is only possible among humans, no other form of living exists beyond biological procedures, and, in fact, that nothing can think, move, live, will, or have awareness and intentions in the whole extent of existence except our own species. An acme of egotism apart, the demands on human credulity of an absolutely atheistical creed are virtually past calculation. Positively and insistently to reject the slightest possibility of "other-living" than within the small limits of mortal experience takes an intensity of belief unreachable by the vast majority of mankind. No one strains harder at gnats or swallows larger camels than a dedicated and devoted atheist. Strangely enough, it seldom occurs to him that his strenuous denial of all extra-mundane existence derives principally from his deliberate refusal to accept its possibility. He may prefer to suppose his atheism results from his intellectual experiences and whatever else he accepts as evidence, but if he were honest he would have to admit limits to his capacity of consciousness. Within those limits his denials are legitimate to himself alone, but past that mark others are entitled to what experiences they will.

It is quite reasonable for anyone to say in effect: "Within my experience and understanding no other types of conscious life or entity exist than those inside my range of intellect and comprehension. Such is my sincere belief". That is not atheism but a simple admission of self-limitation. It would also be fair to say: "I refuse to concern myself with other than human limits of living". That is an entitlement of free will which is our natural birth-right. Or someone could equally say: "I admit such things may be, but I would rather have nothing to do with them". That again is entirely a matter of personal decision or opinion. The crux of the whole issue is one of recognition or admission that what are now called paranormal conditions of conscious entity are conceivable as concomitants of our cosmos. This is all. Once such a stand- point is made, the second basic belief behind magic becomes possible. What follows from thence (if anything) will depend entirely on the people or circumstances concerned.

The third basic of relationship between intelligent humans and "energy-entities" usually inaccessible to most mortals, may almost automatically be considered as a possibility once the first two basics prove acceptable. We are not asking here whether or not this should occur, be a good or bad practice, how it might be done, or anything beyond its conceivability. If relationships of any kind at all, however remote, are possible between embodied mortals and non-incarnates of whatever category, then magic becomes at least theoretically workable, and translation of theory into practice is generally only an affair of application through adequate conditions of development.

The very moment that magic amounts to an admissible possibility, almost endless questions arise to be answered. Is it worth while or not, beneficial or otherwise, difficult or easy, and what is its methodology? Those are some of the most immediate points presented to inquirers. There is also the overriding query of why bother with any form of "inner agency" at all? Why can't we do what we want by ourselves? The straight answer to this, of course, is that if we had such capabilities we should be higher than humans, anyway. If, while yet human, we insist on making intentional demands of life none of our facilities are able to supply, then we have no alternative but to direct those demands towards whatever agency seems most likely to deal equitably with them. It does not follow in the least that our initial intentions will eventuate as specified, or even seem to have had any effect whatever outside the originator's awareness. So much depends upon the "inner agencies" concerned, and a wide variety of factors outside our competence to control. On the other hand, it is amazing what may be accomplished through such agencies, making allowances for natural factors of time-space- events comprising our cosmic continuum.

Mankind as a whole has always realised those possibilities one way or another. Whether by means of elaborate sacrifices to God-concepts, placation of dreaded demons, charms, spells and conjurations, or straight- forward prayers to saints and divinities, humans have placed problems beyond their power of solution in whatever "higher hands" they believed upon all down the ages. As often as not those problems were either answered or ultimately equated. Very seldom by any sort of unusual intervention with natural laws, most eventuating through normal, though often unexpected, channels. In the course of evolution, as man has learned how to solve more and more of his most pressing problems for himself by his own ingenuity, so have the responses of "inner agencies" appeared to recede into those more abstract realms which we have not yet managed to manoeuvre for ourselves. We seem to have been "led along" as it were, by our attempts to contact spheres of consciousness lying somewhat beyond whatever range of awareness we presently possess. No matter how far we progress, it is always that immediately unknown area just ahead of us which calls us with unmistakable clarity along our "cosmic course". That is the area in which we are most likely to make our closest contacts with inner intelligences interested in helping us evolve into increasingly higher levels of living. Therefore we shall focus our attention on that point and see what follows.

The first obvious factor is what we might call the "validity value" of the inner contact we seek. That is to say, whether or not our original purpose is likely to meet even the slightest response from any spiritual sort of agency. For instance, we should have no hope at all of any magic immediately materializing some demanded objective. Yet magic may subtly start a chain of events commencing with consciousness and culminating in concrete form through appropriate channels. It is a question of energy conversion. There is a formula for converting energy between physical and spiritual dimensions, but it will not help greedy opportunists very greatly. It is expressed:

$$\text{C.I.} \quad \frac{Q \ + \ A}{S \ + \ M} = \text{E.}$$

Q	=	Quality
A	=	Amount
S	=	Skill
M	=	Means
I	=	Intention
C	=	Constant
E	=	Effect

Here we see that the factors o f *quality* and *amount* are divisible by available *skill* and *means,* the whole being related by a *constant* being applied *intentionally* through- out the equation to produce an eventual effect. In our external cosmos the *constant* is light, and in our inner cosmos it is the mystical equivalent of light, or *illumination.*

From .this formula it is obvious that if the C factor is slight the remainder will be insignificant of issue. Also no human being alone could produce a sufficient amount of spiritual energy out of its own private capacity to make much of an end effect. Hence the need for contact with inner sources of supply. Then again, the *intention* factor is an awkward one. For any human to make this great enough for satisfactory results, it would have to be augmented very considerably by other intentions in agreement, or extended perhaps a great deal through time until an adequate build-up occurred. Magic is not just a matter of wand-waving but of co-ordinating all necessary points of a power-plan related with purpose.

In general, therefore, we may expect that the spiritual factors employed in magic will operate through purely inner fields of force, only affecting our material condition where direct linkage is available. Assuming a validity of intention and correct constant of consciousness, there is every reason to suppose the other factors are likely to be augmented from inner supplies by responsible agencies. What, then, seems to be the most valid intention a human being might have in this world? The conversion of evil into good? Strange to say not entirely, because good can be perverted back into evil again by contrary intentions. To convert evil into good *and then equate both principles into a poised perfection,* is the highest, holiest and surely the most valid intention possible to humans hoping for ultimate emancipation into infinite enlightenment. It is the "transmutation" of Hermeticists, which signifies establishment of the "Golden Mean" pillar between the extremities of the black and white ones.

This takes us back to the legend of our "fall" or accepting responsibility of choice between good or evil. It is the very convertibility of these principles in our world which indicates how far we have fallen from original potential perfection. The very best of all we consider good, and the worst of what we accept as evil is impermanent and alternative. Each principle automatically implies the other. As affairs stand with humanity in mundane conditions we cannot work good unless evil existed, nor could we work evil unless its opposite principle made it so. Each creates the other's possibilities. That is the position we have arrived at since partaking of the fatal fruit obtained from the Tree of Knowledge. In other words, the development of our intellect and experience has very greatly increased our scope for both good and evil. Only the Tree of Life can produce the inner qualities we need for equating everything into a stable spiritual cosmic condition by the middle pillar connecting us directly with that super-supernal state termed *perfect peace profound.* This amounts to the "redemption" of mankind into the immortal status of identity intended originally by our Eternal Initiator.

Therefore, in designing any kind of magical rite or practice to incorporate and relate all these factors, we must bear in mind the fundamental pattern of the whole spiritual structure. This is simple enough in essence. We need to take our starting situation and project it through its evil or worst possibilities into infinite negation, pull back the good and best possibilities from the other side until it levels with us, then raise up the "pillar of perfect poise" between the two extremes which connects us directly with whatever we accept as divinity. By this act we identify our own wills with that of the eternal entity operating through us. If we can make a satisfactory symbolic and dramatized version of all this, it should prove of the greatest spiritual help. By "acting out" our problems with co-ordinated hearts, minds, souls and spirits, their solutions are bound to eventuate through the inner energies which will become set in motion thereby.

Ritual psycho-dramas are usually enacted in a "temple" or special area set up for this sole purpose. Their vital inner patterns, however, should apply to life itself on all intended levels. That is to say, what we do or say symbolically in our temples must be capable of translation into other terms of living both in physical and more subtle spheres. Otherwise a rite would be no more than private theatricals. It is the extensibility of a rite into life which is of paramount importance. That is the keynote of sound ritualism. Once any rite is successfully "temple-set", its performance in terms of inner or outer living should become perfectly practical and normal. The function of a temple is similar to a research laboratory which develops prototype specimens of important items intended for much wider fields of application. Temples ought to be for producing "life-patterns" which will eventuate according to intention. The advantage of temple-work is that it affords favourable conditions for humans to co-operate with other types of entities whose capabilities of consciousness are very different from ours. Our natural interests should be to establish linkage with those inner or "spiritual" beings who are most closely concerned with our highest and best possibilities of life in its supreme sense. This is accomplished by mutual intentions and patterns of partnership. Quite possible outside a physical temple, of course, but such a starting point is undeniably useful and convenient as a basis for building the true temple "not made with hands" which has to be constructed inside ourselves where the actual inner contacts are made.

Temple ritualism works by means of physical, verbal and other co-ordinated symbology which forms a framework for the equivalent energies employed. It is best to keep these carefully confined to essentials only. Whatever is not part of the pattern should not intrude into the rite. Apart from temple working space, the physical elements of this particular rite are very simple. Two practical pillars (black and white), a central staff (gold or otherwise}, plus a symbolic overhead contact between the pillars with a central zero significance, and a floor-level symbolic linkage with a central base for erecting the staff. All this can be easily contrived from hardboard and wooden uprights coloured with ordinary enamel paint. For those without their own ideas, the two pillars may be about seven feet high, minimum of an inch thick, standing on made-up bases or in earth-pots, connected at bottom by a flat foot-wide strip of grey material and across the top by an arched strip to represent the rainbow, violet at the white pillar and red at the black. The yellow central point of this hopeful spectrum may be zero-shaped or, better still, have a hole in which a point of actual light appears. The pillars are best about 32 inches (81.3 cm) apart. A thin gold-painted rod at least as tall as the ritualist should be ready to erect centrally in some special symbolic base or an ordinary earth-pot placed centrally between the pillars on the grey strip connecting them on the floor.

The mime-mechanics of the rite are again easy. It all begins with the ritualist facing the pillars at a distance of the gilt staff which is lying exactly between them on the floor. Directing attention at the central base-point, the operator visualizes or otherwise concentrates on whatever issue is being dealt with. The earth-point or central base represents this problem or other concern *as it appears or seems to the operator as an intelligent human being.* A Qabalist would say its Malkuthic or mundane form. There are obviously only two main issues of this, a best or a worst as may be judged by the rite-worker. These are invoked one after the other in this way. First, the problem or point of the rite is focussed into clear consciousness and associated with the central "here-now" bottom base between the pillars. This is carried over to the black pillar and the worst issues imagined, visualized, and otherwise dwelt on while the focus of attention travels steadily up the pillar. As this ascent is made, possibilities should be made worse and worse until the top of the pillar is reached at a point where nothing can possibly seem more black or dreaded. Now comes the all-important "push- off" process of negating or neutralising it all.

This begins with the realisation that no matter how bad things may become there has to come an end somewhere beyond which they just cease altogether because we ourselves have been pushed past that point into a condition of "unreaction" or "nothingness" wherein they cannot affect us adversely. Physically this may mean our deaths, but spiritually it signifies having reached a release point into a state of "universal ultimation". Qabalists would say we had entered the "Ain-Soph-Aur" of infinite nil or zoic zero. Mystics might call it "passing into peace profound", and Christians could term the condition "being gathered into God". However we nominate the spiritual state we are symbolically seeking here, its significance is that of having gone beyond all human limits along a specified path (in this case that of the worst possibilities related to a particular problem) and reaching a point where the whole issue can be dealt with by a much more capable consciousness than our own. Such a "cosmic competence" is obviously quite able to take this stream of energy we are directing into it, neutralize the forms of its force into zero potential, then re-issue it all out again in an entirely opposite way. In childish language "God can turn bad into good – if we ask Him properly".

So having made out matters to be so bad we cannot possibly conceive them worse, we push them off the black pillar at the top altogether, and along the upper arc to its centre-point where they should be seen as going out of our cognisance entirely into whatever infinite identity we accept as being inconceivable by our pathetically limited consciousness. If a colour spectrum is used, we may visualize the fierce red flames of torment changing down through orange into a beautifully glowing light of a beneficent sun shining for the sake of cosmic comfort and "limitless life". Into the "utterly unknown sun behind the sun" we must keep pushing all the fearsomeness we have raised so far with the voiced or unvoiced plea for transformation into its equivalent opposite. In a sense, this is not unlike the Christian custom of "offering up one's sufferings to God". The practice calls for great concentration and aim, somewhat resembling the attitude of a marksman lining up sights upon a target. Zen archery practice is a good example of what is needed here. A dedicated aim offered utterly and unreservedly to the ultimate aim of life itself operating through the human archer. A total transference of will from the human to the divine end of an entity.

When the sense of "entry" into the neutral nil-point of balance between the pillars has been achieved to maybe some slight degree, an emergence of energy having an opposite polarity and proceeding toward and down the white pillar should be called to consciousness. On the colour scale it may be at first gloriously gold, then peacefully green, and lastly splendidly blue, fading to ultra-violet as it blends into the white of the pillar. Now we can see the prospects of our original problem getting all the way down the pillar until by the time we have reached the bottom starting point nothing could possibly be more to our estimation of its greatest good. Another *ne plus ultra* has been arrived at, this time in terms of what we believe might be possible in our mundane "here- now" if divinity itself intervened in our favour.

It is maybe tempting to leave the process at that and hope for fulfilment of such wishful thinking, but this would be a very futile and silly thing to do. We should know that these best possibilities invoked have no more permanence in cosmic continuity and constancy than their worst opposites. What we really need is an absolutely balanced relationship with the central source of spiritual power exactly between and above all living awareness and action. We need to so rise above the goods and evils of human existence that we shall live only by and for the "central cosmic principle of perfect poise", or the "correct course" which, when found, leads humanity toward divinity. Sometimes this is called "the strait and narrow way"; Buddha defined it as "selfless rightness"; and Qabalists refer to the "middle line" or most direct and exact connection between the human and divine ends of an entity. Whatever it is, it amounts to a dedicated sense of balanced being and continuity extending not only through extremities of a single life-time, but right through an entire existence of indefinite evolution.

Once this was considered to be submission of human will to a divine intention. Perhaps a broader view is that we become enabled to fulfil our own proper purposes as directed by the intention responsible for our existence as entities in the first place. However the issue is considered, it adds up to living and being as we should in accordance with our "maker's instructions" invisibly yet indelibly printed on the base of our most secret selves. This is something quite apart from what we might want or feel like at any given "here-now" of our mortal manifestations. Materially we are a mass of mutables, but our spiritual basics reach a stable permanence in the "perfect peace" behind our beings. Identification with that would mean immortality. Therefore we need to connect our consciousness with the ultimate point by means of the "light-line" or golden rule which is symbolized by the slender staff lying on the floor centrally between the bases of the pillars and our feet at its other end.

There are several ceremonial ways of "raising the

rod". A gracefully significant one is by first kneeling on both knees so that the end may be grasped by both hands, then a rise is made while gripping the staff, first on the left leg, then the right. The staff is then raised in position by walking steadily forward as the hands alternate down it. At final position the staff should be fixed in its base and lined up with centre top precisely between the pillars. The hands may still clasp the staff at about middle point if desired. The symbology of this act should explain itself. We seek our highest aim by kneeling humbly before the Supreme Spirit and consequently find what we should at our very feet. If we grasp this slender standard firmly enough, it will assist us to rise from lowest levels into an upright and firm-standing position of poise. Moreover, it will point our way quite clearly to our highest ultimate aim.

All that kind of thinking should be followed and developed while the staff is being raised between the pillars. When finally positioned, it represents the ritualist himself in perfect balance with every opposed energy of existence to be experienced within the force-framework of the pillars. The ideal spiritual stance to be adopted in all cosmic contingencies. Once the staff is in its final position, a comparably poised inner attitude should be arranged by the ritualist. The aim should be to arrive at a sense of acceptance and agreement with whatever will steer our lives equably between their best or worst possibilities and lead us most directly toward infinite illumination. This was once put: "Not my will, but Thy will in me be done". A few moments of appreciation or reflection at this stage of the rite would not be amiss.

Such then are the bare bones of this somewhat remarkable rite. It amounts to a practical exercise of relationship with life circumstances and the supreme spirit in which all exists. At first it takes time, effort and equipment to organize. Once the pattern and procedure is firmly established in the operator's consciousness it will begin to condition reactions towards living on all levels. Eventually the artificial props and aids of temple arrangements and equipment will become unnecessary for the extension of the exercise into any other life-field. We should prove able to live the rite as a normal activity in terms of applied principles at any given moment. That is the whole idea behind ritualism. First we set up a carefully constructed framework for spiritual energies in suitably symbolic conditions. Then we work at this conscientiously until it ultimates into a state of actuality along intended life-levels. As we operate in our temples so should we subsequently live and eventuate. A true temple is a "life-laboratory" for determining ourselves as we should be if the original intention behind us as individuals is to be realised.

When this solid spiritual function of temple activities is fully understood and appreciated, ritualistic practices take on an entirely new and vital meaning for those best able to use them effectively. All the basic behaviours and appurtenances associated with specific verbal symbology are seen as a means of coded communication between otherwise ordinary mortals and types of consciousness which are not normally observably intrusive into our mundane affairs. In this case we are using this "life-language" to obtain the co-operation of that "inner intelligence" in helping us align ourselves correctly between whatever extremities we are likely to encounter in connection with our specified subject.

Strictly speaking, it is best for everyone to work out

the verbalization and arrangements of his own rites once the general pattern and lay-out is determined and agreed upon. However, for those finding difficulty with such details, here follows a ritual script which covers all the areas we have been considering. Most of it is in succinct rhymed meter in order to condense the necessary consciousness into suitable force-foci. Unnecessary and pointless verbosity in ritual work is a bad fault leading to little but boredom and disillusionment. Every single word and phrase should be so charged with meaning and power of purpose that it may even be difficult for the operator to enunciate them adequately while attempting to appreciate their significance. Assuming the properties and symbols for the rite have been correctly set up, it may open with the sign of the Cosmic Cross thus:

In the Name of the Wisdom (touch forehead]

And of the Love (touch heart]

And of the Justice (right shoulder]

And the Infinite Mercy (left shoulder]

Of the one Eternal Spirit (clockwise complete circle covering those points and finish centre]

Amen (Join hands prayer position]

1. Indicating all the symbols, say and mean:

> **Be this a pattern of My (our) present problem/s and**.........
> **The sure solution**..........
> **In and by the Light of Living Truth.**

2.Focus attention on bottom centre-base symbol and say with meaning:

Become for Me (us) a symbol of [whatever is intended]
And all associated links in life.

After this has been clearly conceived, continue:
We (I) shall now see
What more might be.

3. Move attention to the Black Pillar and invoke:
Let bad and worse appear
With every ill We (I) fear.

4. Here work attention steadily up the Black Pillar, visualizing all possible misfortunes or ills connected with the subject of the Rite. These should seem worse and worse as the Pillar is mentally mounted. When they seem beyond all endurance utter dramatically:

Sufferance cease there!
That is enough to bear.
Now into utmost nil.
May dreads be driven still.

5. Attention is now directed to top centre and a sense sought of all those dreadful contingencies being neutralised and passed back into a peaceful state of pure spiritual potential. There should be nothing left behind except a condition of "trustful tranquillity". The action is directed verbally.

Be nothing. Cease!
Find perfect peace.
By living light
Be all made right.

6. When a state of suitable equation is experienced begin to call out a continuation of the original energy, but this time pass over to the White Pillar top and start to see everything in a much better light. Initiate this process by saying:

Come forth from rest
As good and best.

7. Follow this trend carefully down the White Pillar while prospects improve almost impossibly all the way until bottom is reached. Realise that in this world such extremes are most improbable, so halt there and kneel by the end of the staff on the floor. Verbalize:

Let this suffice to show
The most we (I) hope to know.
Now may a middle line
Link us (me) with light divine.

8. Raise self and staff firmly with intention of uniting the individual will with Universal Will. Mean this with all possible purpose. Make this act as deliberate and careful as ability allows. Line up the staff as if it were an ultra-accurate micrometer measure and the difference between total failure or success of everything depended entirely on the delicacy of this action and calculation. Say very carefully:

Whatever life can bring
Through this specific thing
Above all may that be
As true wills shall agree.

While that is being said raise the attention from the symbol of the rite-subject at base (which should hold the earth end) of the staff.

9. Holding the staff about centre, see the whole scheme complete and balanced. Realize this is the best way to live and say confidently:

Between extremes of worst and best
May I (we) stand equalized and blest
By all that lies within my (our) scope
Of living for my (our) highest hope.

10. Stand back and contemplate what has been done, resolving to carry it out on deepest conscious levels with the help of those who link in there. Sum up:

So may I (we) ever be
From good and ill set free
To live by blessed light
And stay in truth upright.
In the Name of the Wisdom
And of the Love
And of the Justice
And the Infinite Mercy
Of the one Eternal Spirit
Amen.

Such is an economically workable temple presentation of this rite. Of course it can be made as elaborate as anyone might prefer by the addition of music, incense or other ritual adjuncts. The only rule about these is that they would be permissible providing they assisted the consciousness of the operator and participants (if any) *in direct connection with the central objective.* Otherwise not. Nothing whatever should be "put in for fun" or "just as an experiment", or any such motive at all. That might be possible with other types of ritual, but positively not in this instance. The whole keynote of this rite depends upon exactness and precision in making the most delicate of all decisions, how to relate oneself directly with divinity despite every other possibility. Therefore its structure has to be accordingly arranged.

With practice it is possible to reduce the verbal components of the rite to a basic four words after the objective or purpose has been clearly called to consciousness and nominated. From that point on, the ritualist need only say:

Worst (black pillar)
Least (upper ultimate zero)
Best (white pillar)
Just (central connection).

By the use of such an elementary formula, the rite could be successfully worked in the mind at any time or condition of mundane circumstances. To achieve this expertise, however, prior temple practice proves an enormous advantage. There is no doubt at all that suitable temples can create favourable "womb-conditions" for gestating spiritually what will then become projected into life on other intended levels. It must never be forgotten, however, that the real temples are "sacred spaces with symbols" consecrated and constructed *within one's inner being*. Physical temples, no matter how mystical and magical, are only guides and suggestions towards that end.

Magical rites may not seem very effective when read in cold print, nor may they appear all that impressive when performed or participated in. Once their patterns penetrate deeply enough beneath the surface levels of mundane living, however, experience will show that considerable effects are produced in actualities of existence. A major effect of this particular rite is of stabilizing and regulating whole life attitudes by a standard system of simple self-adjustments. This alone would be sufficient to cause many favourable changes in the make-up of most mortals and their circumstances. To alter ourselves is always the best move to make first if we intend to alter our conditions. If in addition, we have favourable force- flows from other entities of superior spiritual status, then so much the better for us eventually. Now we need to shift our viewpoint from these considerations to another angle altogether and see how the problems of dealing with good and evil look from that line of investigation. We might be led to some very interesting discoveries.

Chapter Five

Balancing Out

Possibly one of the most significant lines from Goethe's *Faust* is Mephistopheles' description of his own nature. He says:

… I am part of that power – misunderstood – which always evil wills, yet ever worketh good.

The enigma here is how a devil could possibly come to work good against its natural inclination. Whether or not such good would prove as ephemeral as the evil it converted from is not the point at issue. The implication behind the lines is that no matter how evil our affairs of life may be, sooner or later everything is bound to be for the best. No consolation whatever for those in states of suffering, but at least some foundation for faith in an ultimate intention of perfection behind all our being and becoming.

To observe reflections of this principle in action we need only examine characteristics of human behaviour over the centuries. Yesterday's "baddies" become today's "goodies" despite so many of their efforts to the contrary. Once the old robber barons had pillaged, murdered, savaged and otherwise ill-treated their fellow humans into subservient support of the feudal system, they began to alter their outlook through succeeding generations. Their descendants eventually became a controlling class within a much wider social system, which circumstances forced them to share with those who challenged their superiority along very different angles of approach. It now seemed that the lineal inheritors of the bold bad barons' ill-gotten gains had become the staunchest supporters of law, order, state, church and other respected institutions. In fact, few people turn more respectable than reformed revolutionaries. The criminals of one century convert into the conforming citizens of the next. Not for any particularly noble motivation, but generally to support their superior social status. In the course of this change a great many evils are bound to alter with advantage for many involved with the immediate pattern of procedures.

Perhaps an excellent example of all this can be found in contemporary history of "big-time" American crime. Before World War II, economic and social disturbances in the United States resulted in the successful emergence of a ruthless and determined criminal element who fought their way into control positions of finance and influence by similar methods to old-time robber barons extrapolated into the present century. Once these challengers of reputed legality had obtained their main objectives their incentives altered accordingly. To cover their criminal activities they purchased and set up acceptably legitimate businesses, only to discover that the profits on these could far outstrip their wildest expectations of illegitimate avarice. An elaborate operation to rob a bank of a million dollars in cash would be a hazardous and difficult undertaking for many experts, whose distributed profits after discount, etc, might only be a small percentage apiece. On the other hand, if a wide chain of grocery stores were owned, a few cents on items purchased by all consumers would amount to many millions of dollars profit in a very short time. Where hardworking crime could earn cents, computerized commodity selling would rake in untold dollars more or less for the asking. All it needed was organisation and elimination of serious competitors.

When the hierarchs of this modern-style invisible "empire" were successfully established in positions of almost unassailable power, expansion of their influence became virtually a matter of mere mechanics. Like their baronial predecessors, they aspired to aristocracy with a capital A. Their children were sent to the most expensive education institutions; they recruited the best brains for the highest pay and employed every possible means of securing and enhancing their status over the widest possible areas. In fact, the general outlines of the picture are too well recognized to bear much repetition. What may not be so well appreciated is the "off-loading" of surplus profits in terms of advantages shared by maybe millions of people.

To keep the top structure of such a social network going, vast quantities of improvements had to be made on lower levels. More people must have greater purchasing power in order to push up profits. Their educational standards have to be raised considerably so that increasingly complicated methods and mechanisms may be correctly operated. Health has to be maintained for the sake of output. Strange as it seems, the words of Mephistopheles work out in practice to show that what began in this world with ill intentions of relatively few people usually produced overall side-effects of benefit to many in the long run. When we think of the medical advances made out of human sufferings in world wars, and other instances of very ill winds blowing eventual benefits in different directions, we can appreciate how good effects may be derived from evilly intended events. Unhappily, the converse is also true, and our roads to hell are indeed paved with the best of intentions. We have only to look at the Christian Church for an illustration of this. Founded upon ideas of love, compassion, fellowship of humanity with divinity, and the highest of other motivations, its sad history is reproachfully full of contrary activities. Goethe might have paraphrased his lines to suit some angelic character with the words:

... I am part of that power – misunderstood – which seems to Evil cause when I intended Good.

In fact, with this confusing world it is a moot point whether we owe more of our evils to the well-meaning, and our benefits to the ill-intentioned than the other way about. No wonder we are such mixed-up mortals.

Perhaps one of the oddest factors involved here is the strange insistence of materially "successful" wrongdoers on assuming as much appearance of rectitude as may be purchased with a percentage of their profits. They do not mind actually being bad in themselves so long as other humans are prepared to accept a good image of them. It is almost as if they were willing to work evil for the sake of looking good. Furthermore, this seems to be the general trend among humans. How many people work surreptitiously for good because they want to make an impression of evil on others? Certainly no one with a grain of sanity in their make-up. So why should it only be the other way round for the majority of mankind?

Mainly because most humans know well enough in their own depths what they should be as *selves,* even though they prefer pushing interests of pseudo-self in place of that priority. However much they deny any such thing intellectually, the difference between what they should have been and what they have done with them-selves causes great disquiet and spiritual discontent. So they seek a substitute image of something they might have been if the best part of themselves had only been in unquestioned command of their life-activities among fel-low mortals. Hypocrisy? Partly, perhaps. Wishful thin-king? Maybe. A pathetic pretence of a plea for another chance along other lines of life? One hopes so, because this does show signs, however slight, that humanity as a whole really has something worth working with in the long run, no matter how long such a run is likely to be. That is all we truly need to know for certain in order to in-spire faith in our spiritual fulfilment. The smallest sign of our mightiest meaning. Nothing less is likely to encour-age our efforts at evolution between the pillars of polarity on the Tree of Life.

We shall not be much helped, either, by classifying all we term good and claiming this associates exclusively with a directing divinity called "God", while we contrast this with its oppositional amount of evil and link it with another (if lesser) spiritual entity named "the Devil". If "God" is All, then the "Devil" has to be another part of "God" divided against its better intentions – which scarcely makes very good sense. If we disassociate "God" from evil, then we must also disclaim any possibilities of good ensuing from the malicious inclinations of "the Devil". As we have seen, the opposing principles, while being quite apart from each other, are yet convertible through a common cosmic agency. Does this mean that our concepts of "God" and "Devil" are interchangeable, depending on our intentions? Not at all. It means that we need a different and more advanced concept of divinity al-together. Something which elevates our awareness of a supreme spiritual entity far above limits of good or evil as we recognize these principles from our purely human viewpoint. Such a single spirit of life can have but one central or cosmic principle. Our nearest name for it would be *"perfection"*.

This means to say that a fair definition of divinity would be that *spirit* in everyone and everything which makes all become as initially and ultimately intended by that infinite identity with which the whole of being belongs. We might otherwise say that divinity is what causes everything to become what it should be. Exactly what such a state may be we are yet in the process of learning as we live and evolve toward that very distant seeming point of perfection. However much we are entitled to speculate about this theoretical condition, we can only be certain that it will not be reached in this world as a physical phenomenon. Here, we may only expect perfection to mean the most possible according to our life-limits imposed by the laws of our mundane natures. To progress beyond that extent we should have to become other types of beings living in quite different kinds of dimensions. Since we are so very far from reaching that remote point of liberation from earth-life, we need scarcely worry about it unduly. What matters most is recognition of divinity as an implanted instinct in ourselves to become the very best possible species of our kind in all existence – whatever this may be both in individual and total terms.

No one in his right mind would suppose this process of perfection to be instantaneous, effortless, or otherwise ready-made in terms of our time-space-event sort of existence. Nor need we be consciously aware of its technical details in any objective way. A flower needs no knowledge to know how to become beautiful, and we live in highly organized animal bodies which function very well without our intentional interference with their complex life-systems. It should be obvious that the very limited extent and conditions of life available for humans confined to this planet cannot possibly be sufficient for individuals to reach a required perfection-point within the life-span of one mortal body alone. Hence the necessity for re-embodiment of entities failing to achieve that spiritual standard. Just as there is a physical "escape velocity" for quitting the orbital influence of this earth, so is there a spiritual equivalent permitting a "passage to higher spheres of life". Otherwise we tend to remain "in orbit" as it were, still associating with this biological base we have not risen above sufficiently in spirit to leave for better living systems elsewhere.

Faced with our three-way options for dealing with this divinely inherent instinct in us to perfect ourselves as living beings of our species we can either a) Work with it. b) Let it be. c) Work against it.

On the very broadest of bases the first is a "good" course, the second an ordinary one, and the third an "evil" or "anti-cosmic" outcome. Most people alternate between all three during their lives, ending with a balance which might classify in any category. The vast majority of humans are somewhere about the middle of the scale, responding very slowly and often painfully to their inherited impulses toward an eventual point of perfection. Provided they are prepared to keep pushing in a general direction towards divinity for one generation after another indefinitely they will certainly "get there in the end". If, on the other hand, individual entities refuse to continue in existence they will be entirely negated into new energies and other beings take their place. There is a teaching to the effect that every human soul "dropping out" of our life-chain retards the rest of us by that amount, but conversely every soul "making it" into ultimate entity and *perfect peace* helps our whole life-process accordingly.

Very, very few souls indeed could be called purely good or evil. Those in whom one of these principles preponderates to marked degrees over the other are likely to be found at either the top or bottom ends of human society considered as a species in various stages of development. Extreme examples of "goodies" and "baddies" are generally encountered among very crude and primitive people or else very highly bred and intelligently evolved individuals. It scarcely needs saying that the latter type are far the most dangerous to humanity if they opt for evil. Primitives may be crude and cruel, vicious, destructive, and senselessly violent, but they injure physically and mentally more than spiritually as a rule, and even the worst of their nastiness has definite limits, bad as these may be. In the case of the "top brass" bad-hats, however, a cultivated and continued dedication to really sophisticated forms of evil produces a far more adverse effect upon spiritual areas of the human psyche than the most barbarous brutalities wantonly aimed at smashing bodies.

Both top and bottom types of "baddie" are motivated by the same drive which amounts to aggrandisement of pseudo-self in opposition to the inner impulse toward spiritual perfection. This was once called "disobedience to God's will". However we term it, what seems to happen is a split in our self-systems between an inbuilt inherency to perfect our species as intended by our life-origin, and an impulse to individuate at much lesser levels regardless of method or consequence. Let us be quite clear about this issue, because it is a very important consideration.

We are creations whose initial function is individuation. To that end we are equipped with a sort of spiritual "homing device" which has the "self-circuit" intended to direct all our energies through indefinite incarnations toward that ultimate aim. If it bleeped in English it would constantly call, "Be yourself. Be yourself." Meaning, of course, the *self* intended by its divine designer. It is therefore our most basic instinct and deepest life-drive. Provided we are purely spiritual beings living under totally different conditions of cosmos, this drive would work directly and normally enough. As humans living in biologically bred bodies, however, the story is quite different. The individuation instinct is still very much in evidence, but its possible divergencies have increased almost incredibly. Let us put it this way. If we lived in a state of being wherein only divinity and ourselves existed, we should have to "home in" correctly on our "true target" because no other course was open. Since we live in fact among so many alternative courses how can we be sure to select the right one intended for each one of us? That is the problem we all face constantly. There are so many wrong ways of being our *selves* that it is perhaps scarcely surprising some people prefer to select one of these and make up a "pseudo-self", which is often the entire antithesis of what was originally intended. Those who do this consistently and consciously are diverging toward the evil side of the Tree to whatever degree corresponds with the incidence of their deliberately varied intentions.

To simplify again, let us suppose we are in a spacecraft

which is in constant contact with "mission control", but has full manual optional control also. The craft is set and commissioned for a definite and specific purpose. Now let us imagine the commander of this craft to develop a personal divergence for any reason at all with the originating intention behind the whole mission. Perhaps he is bored. Maybe he thinks he can improve on the idea, or sees what he supposes a short cut. Whatever the motivation may be, he switches the controls to manual and directs his craft towards its altered target. One assumes he turns off or tunes down any protest and remarks from Mission Control received on his radio link. In this analogy there are again three possibilities. Such a policy might improve upon the terms of his original mission, keep harmlessly and effectively within them, or entirely abnegate and misapply them. So indeed is it with humans who by their "fall" into realms of good and evil have deliberately taken their destiny into their own hands and made themselves responsible for their ultimate entitisation or extinction as living souls deriving their existence from infinite spirit.

Our choice between good and evil, therefore, depends entirely upon how we intend "setting up in business for ourselves" as relatively independent "cells of creation". This again ties in with our levels of intelligence and facilities of consciousness which are normally commensurate with evolution. At the crude end of the scale, which is scarcely much above animal level, pseudo-self assertion is generally violence and aggression on the evil side, or gentleness and amiability on the good. As awareness and experience expands consciousness through successive incarnations, however, those early methods alter very much indeed. Intelligence converts aggressive tendencies into authoritarian and other forms of dictatorship while also instigating clever and subtle schemes for coercive control of social situations. On the other side of the picture it guides the basics of gentle amicability into compassionate concern for living creation and an interest in bringing the benefits of advancing culture and civilization to bear upon universal well-being.

The point at issue here is that neither "goodies" nor "baddies" are faithfully following their "maker's instructions", but both are setting up independent establishments, so to speak, for their own specifications of automatic self-government. There are no rights or wrongs to this, but simply unfulfilment of "creation conditions" in each case. Each category by itself if extrapolated to extremes would produce an impasse nothing short of annihilation could possibly clear out of cosmos. The "baddies" would make a hell so awful it would destroy them as well when it reached "critical mass", and the "goodies" would make a heaven so self-sacrificing that no-one would be left to enjoy its amenities. Both would negate themselves in their own fashion if their counter-continuance did not assure a mutual field of existence.

What we need most of all as individual and collective humans is to find the "precise path" which leads our lives clearly and exactly between the principles of good and evil alike so that we direct our cosmic courses according to the divine inherent intention in each and all of us. Whether we call this the "will of God", our own "true wills", it amounts to the same thing – our "best becoming". Whatever it may be it is most certainly some- thing we shall have to find for ourselves within ourselves because it is our *selves* in the real sense of the word.

From time immemorial in this world there have been traditions, religions, systems, secret schools of initiation, sacred mysteries, and all sorts of contrived patterns of symbolic consciousness aimed at this one point of helping human souls to find them-*selves*. Their value cannot be denied until the fatal doctrine of: "We are right and the rest are all wrong. With us you are saved and with them you are damned!" makes it ugly appearance. All that any of these associations could or can fairly claim is to provide facilities for human souls to seek salvation according with whatever particular "divine design" lies within each "true self" a soul belongs to. Since humans can be categorized into broad and subsequently more selective groupings, it would be quite legitimate to say that specific traditions, schools, etc, are most suited for this, that, or the other type of soul. It is for everyone to find such channels of inner communication for them- selves according to need, yet in the end they will have to find what they are seeking within *themselves* and no- where else. Honest systems of initiation will freely admit this while offering whatever assistance their experience and Inner facilities may make available for fellow mortals. Any special claims or offers of special initiations for payment should be treated with the suspicion they deserve. So should religious claims of exclusive salvation providing generous support is received from subscribing members.

How is anyone to know how to find the Golden Mean between the black and white pillars of their Life-Trees? Though this vital question is virtually unanswerable except as individual realizations, the general indication could be in these terms. By determining a life-course, entirely devoid of personally perceptible profits, which carries a complete conviction of being correct entirely for its own inherent reasons. It was otherwise put: "A thing is not right because God wills it, but God wills it because it is right". The "Gita" reduced the idea to a single instruction: "work uninvolved". The Qabalah illustrates the point by symbolizing its highest concept of divinity as a dignified right-hand profile and the phrase: "He is all right, and in Him there is no left-hand path". In other words, something cosmically correct in itself whether or not anyone other than its originator existed to realize this.

As humans, we can only reach a reflection of this "perfect principle" in that self-state of living consciousness we are confined to on these earth levels. Nevertheless, if reflections are faithfully and, carefully followed with attention they will lead to the reality they represent in the end. That is to say providing we do recognize reflections for what they are and remain ready to alter our attitudes as our advancing awareness comes closer to the actuality in question. The difficulty is that with so many confusing reflections in this world, how are we possibly to pick on the right one leading to ultimate light? Especially when we all have individual leads to look for.

Various systems have advised different specific methods of achieving such awareness. They mainly amount to graduated exercises calculated to establish links between consciousness at incarnation level and subtler states of spiritual sensitivity extended inwardly toward divinity. These are chiefly intended to help users recognize and identify their own particular paths among all the possibilities encountered on earth-life levels and immediate inner associations. As a rule all this sub- classifies into very broad bands of action designed to cover a majority section of humanity, after which these lead into narrower and more specialized channels which again define sharply into points of individual focus. Thus, it is at least theoretically possible for sincere souls to start self-searching in very wide waters so to speak, which will gradually provide currents that diversify in accordance with needs, so that in the end everyone becomes carried along their own closest course to the ultimate destination all may share as *one*.

Although there are so many time-wasting proliferations among all the systems of spiritual and pseudo- spiritual development, there is one factor which can be used like a razor to cut out most of the doubtful elements. That is the presence of a profit motive not only in terms of money, but also of power, advantage over others, or more subtle sort of gain for the sake of pseudo-self aggrandisement. Whatever scheme is concocted to enrich its promoters at the expense of its supporters in any way, is beyond doubt fraudulent so far as spiritual rectitude is concerned. This does not mean it might be legally or even morally wrong in a strict sense, but simply that by its very nature it *cannot* operate, beyond the lowest levels of inner human instincts. Past a certain level of our inner beings, desires and compulsion to amass profits by scheming, greed or other means cease entirely. If those motivations are traceable, then it is safe to assume that they only proceed from less than midway up the spiritual scale we should accept as a standard of human relationships with infinite identity. That is just inadequate for finding our highest sight-lines of true selfhood, and therefore should be transcended in ourselves or in schemes promoted by others.

There is no use suspecting spiritual dishonesty in others

and not recognizing it in ourselves. If, by any chance, we are seeking spiritual advancement in order to get ahead of everyone else, gain advantages, reap fat profits everywhere, and otherwise get into the best positions of earth, heaven, and maybe hell, then we shall be just as guilty as the cheapest crook in search of dollar- constipated suckers. If indeed anyone is merely looking for entertainment and amusement in the fringe areas of human spiritual activities, then it is best to recognise and admit this honestly while remaining within those limits until sufficiently ready to rise higher up the self-scale by the path of perfect poise. Far better admit an unsatisfactory self-state and cope with it clumsily than hypo- critically pretend otherwise for foolish motives of attempted self-deception. The true self is never deceived. Only pseudo-self enjoys personal pretences – while these last.

If only people "shopping around" for spiritual leads to follow towards ultimate truth would face facts sometimes and say: "I don't know what I'm really looking for, so I'm playing with all these pretty things in the hope they might suggest something. I like dressing up and having fun with psychodramas. Intellectual puzzles intrigue me and make me think. Symbols fascinate me, and I just love an incense-laden atmosphere with a lot of rhythmic chanting going on. It may be an expensive hobby, but I think its worth the money – to me at any rate. At all events it seems to fill a need for me and make my life worth going on with. I'm sure it does me good". One honest admission along those lines is worth a thousand specious substitutes and unsuccessful self-deceptions. Moreover, it would make the magic work for such a seeker – probably for the first time.

This is not meant to imply that magical practices lead

no higher than personal profiteering. It means that things must be seen in their proper perspective. Once it is recognized that profit motivations are at the very bottom of our spiritual scale and cannot possibly lead any higher, then it becomes a matter of individual choice whether to remain on those low levels or try above them. If the latter decision is taken, then all expectations of profit must be abandoned right away to leave a clear spiritual space for climbing. "Blessed is he that hopeth for nothing", is no idle phrase, even if a difficult one to grasp. That is exactly what we must hope for in order to set accurate sights on our highest aims. That *perfect peace* which is "nothing" to the greed-grab motivations of our lowest self-levels, yet "all" to the infinite identity we hope will ultimately be ours in total truth.

Be it carefully noted that the term used to describe a principal avoidance-factor in dealing with spiritual systems is "profit", and not "recompense" or "entitlements". All expenditures of energy in existence have a natural entitlement of return or recompense relative to their amounts. That could be described as a "right". What would *not* be either natural or "right" would be expectations of surplus energy in the circuit which could be sequestered to supply another demand. That would be like asking a 10 horse-power motor to work a 100 horse-power dynamo, which in turn should work 10 more such motors. Not even the maddest mechanic would ever dream of such a fantasy, and yet the principle of profiteering on any level makes much crazier demands of human greeds and credulities.

Profiteering implies taking more out of a supply source than is returned and somehow preventing or ignoring such due returns for whatsoever reason. Commercially, this might be demanding higher and higher prices for less and poorer materials while feeding none of those gains back into buyers' pockets from any direction. As we know from history, this inevitably leads to revolutions, breakdowns of society, wars, and other very serious disruptions and calamities. Out of those disasters a new species of profiteer arises, and so the terrible cycle goes on. There are more ways of profiteering than with money, however. Spiritual profiteering is much more subtle and in the end more dangerous to humanity, because it warps souls from one incarnation to another and affects people over very pro- longed periods of their evolutionary progress. While common commercial profiteering is easy to recognize, and greatly to be deplored, its spiritual counterpart may not be so readily perceptible, and therefore is thus more difficult to deal with.

The recognition marks of spiritual greed-grabbers are actually rather similar to those of mere materialists. First, of course, the endless demands upon increasing sup- pliers and a constant insistence on expansion with an obsessional fixation on becoming bigger regardless of effects on others. Then a display of showy "trade-goods" calculated on an appeal basis to the worst or greediest propensities of sucker-customers. Also the heartless exploitation of "not-so-bright" adherents who are willing to part with work, worship and worldly goods in exchange for promises utterly beyond the power of persuaders to fulfil. One might mention the sinister side of applying coercion by means of fear through threats of dire con- sequences upon those failing to toe approved lines smartly enough. Churches, temples, lodges, fraternities and all spiritual systems are constantly being misused in this way by what amounts to spiritual profiteers who frequently expect a material rake-off into the bargain. Those who suffer from the malicious ministrations of such soul-snatchers usually have themselves to blame for being so foolish or so greedy, but this does not help humanity as a whole very greatly.

With all these points in view, it is advisable to check very carefully what one's own motives actually are before presenting oneself before the portals of any Inner Temple and demanding admission. If personal profits are the motive, and all that is expected comes to something like spiritual one-up-manship with a lot of fringe benefits such as pretty costumes, high-sounding titles, decorative accessories, social amenities and the rest of similar rubbish, then those low levels are as much as may be anticipated. If, conversely, what is being sincerely sought is straightforwardly a poised relationship with the only possible perfection in existence as an ultimate entity, or what would have been called a *Man-God* connection, then the position centralizes into an "ask nothing, await all" affair. In mystical language we should say: "Thy will, not mine, be done". Which, of course, is the correct attitude for approaching our highest possible source of *self.*

A religious person might describe this spiritual stance as "Seeking God for God's sake". A mystical practitioner could call it "looking for Identity in Ultimate Entity" or "approaching the Mystical Union". There are many terms purporting to signify what amounts to an "exact equity angle" held between an entity and its own origins of life. In fact, we have no adequate phraseology for it and can only approximate ideas by whatever symbology seems suitable for the purpose. The golden rule or staff exactly between the two pillars of black and white is at least a workable symbol. It does suggest that we should not want to be "goodie" little people rushing around doing all kinds of things which can be converted back into evil afterwards. Nor should we strive to become big bold "baddies" having ourselves a hell of a success on earth which may subsequently be turned to good account by others. Those are both fallible courses to take. The correct, or "right", course of cosmos for anyone is to aim at becoming exactly whom and what is basically intended in itself by the self which intended it to *BE*. The one "yes" between two "no's". The formula might well be put: negate, negate, asseverate. It was once laid out as, "Seek first the rightness of God, then add other things as needed".

If such a cosmic course could be decided upon definitely by sufficient selves operating consciously in this world, there is no doubt we should be living in far better conditions than at present. Since this seems unlikely for a very long time to come, it appears best to concentrate upon individual efforts from those recognising the necessity for such "ultra-altruism". What this amounts to is making a realization which leads to living not for the sake of profits nor pleasantries, but purely for the principles of perfection inherent in everyone. This does not mean we might ever be perfect while actually incarnate here, but what matters is that we live for the principles of our perfection-possibility. This will always keep us pointing in the right direction, however, far we may be from the end in view. That is the really vital factor. So long as we stay "on course" we are sure to reach our truth target eventually. Holding this in consciousness is like keeping the controls of a vehicle steady on whatever mark deter- mines its proper progress. Though there may be even considerable drift on either side of this datum line, the ship of "self" has to reach its right destination ultimately if its correct course is re-set periodically. Naturally, the oftener re-setting is made the less drift will happen.

To a careless viewer, this might seem like an enormous sacrifice of selfish interests in life involving the foregoing of all pleasures, due rewards, and most of what seems to make living in this world endurable. Not so at all. Expended energy is entirely entitled to responsive returns eventually and equitably. The single factor to be avoided is "profit", which is not a fair return at all but virtually energy wrongly appropriated from other channels which consequently unbalances the whole circuit involved. Correct procedure for returns rising past safe tolerance points is to feed these back into their central supply source for redistribution elsewhere as needed. Commercially, this would be "ploughing profits back into the business again" instead of using the money to finance the owner's private pursuits. Spiritually, it means claiming only our cosmic entitlements and allowing all in excess to be re-absorbed into the infinite source of all energy for re-issue otherwise. It equally means that if we are in fact lacking due return of spiritual entitlements we can claim these to balance our beings correctly. What we cannot do by these methods, however, is demand conditions of return in terms of our lower life-level attributions or commodities. Once we have invoked our highest self-source, any returns have to be made from thence according to *intention* on that level, which may not please our incarnated personalities at all.

This point must be fairly borne in mind before attempting any genuine operation of a magical nature. It should be obvious that no one can dictate to the divine end of themselves from a relatively puny human viewpoint. All we can do is make whatever representations seem suitable at this end, line these up with our central control contact, then transfer direction over to the highest end of our entities. After that it becomes an issue of abiding by decisions taken at top levels of life and arranging earthly affairs accordingly. We can at least be sure that resultant returns will be the best possible in relation to our total self-situation over all levels.

All this procedure is normal enough in the nature of our lives anyway, even though it may take prolonged periods to work out. As a rule, humans are not very conscious of its processes, especially if physical death breaks up continuity of consciousness on earth levels. As we develop and evolve, however, we are expected to take a correspondingly greater interest in and assume responsibility for, the guiding factors which are steadily and slowly making us into what we were supposed to become at the inception of our beings. This means our consciousness of at least a fraction of these forces should co-relate with our human circumstances and prove increasingly amenable to control from this level. Once this was simply put: "Thy will be done on earth as it is in heaven". In other words, the human ends of our entities should behave more and more as their divine counterparts intend. A faint beginning in this direction is made consciously when we start intentionally attempting to co-operate with our highest inner contacts linking with cosmic life.

Expressions of such consciousness with us vary a great deal. Some people use words and symbols, others apply their awareness to living in other ways. We are principally concerned in this study with those who habitually use symbol-summations and methods termed magical for concentrating their consciousness into specific channels. So we shall see how this concept of central control of consciousness linked between the human and divine ends of any entity works out in ritualized symbology. We can use our pillar-staff symbols quite well here. To begin with, the staff stands centrally to represent the operator, who takes it firmly at centre and directing attention upwards toward infinite identity asserts:

Thou total truth of me
As I am part of thee,
May one united will
Our mutual life fulfil.

Next the staff is inclined toward the black pillar at the top until it touches, and all possible wrongs and evils which the operator might be guilty of, or capable of doing, or would wish to do are visualized briefly but definitely, and these are then relinquished by the lesser self-levels and offered to the higher with the words:

Take Thou my wrongs
And make them right.
Neutralize them in Thy light.

All those wrongs and their possible effects are then directed into the infinite nil and a few moments of confirmatory contemplation spent. Then all the possible good the operator would like to do on his own account is considered while the staff is pushed over to the white pillar. These again are handed over to the higher will for decision and other inclination released into Infinity with the words:

**Let nothing good come out of me
That is not done by Thy decree.**

After a short contemplation again, the staff is centralized and steadied while the human end of the entity passes up for even a momentary realization of what union with Divinity might mean. The directing formula is:

**Let good and evil in me cease.
Be Thou my life as perfect peace.**

Lastly, a realization is made that man can only be at his best if he expresses his own particular piece of divine intention as well as he may, and so a recognitory resolution is made:

**So far as we are one,
Let will be duly done.
In the Name of the Wisdom
And of the Love
And of the Justice
And the Infinite Mercy
Of the one Eternal Spirit Amen**

That final formula conveys a definite intention of only doing whatever both human and divine ends of entity agree upon in the individual concerned.

This rite can be expanded, of course, or maybe better still shortened down to a very brief form which is only recognizable to those who know the working principles behind it. In this way no actual physical symbols are needed, and the rite may be done on mental and inner levels in a very short time. The verbal components are:

1 **One** [addressing infinity]
2 **Non-evil** [negating evils via black pillar]
3 **Ultra-good** [negating good via white pillar]

4 Divine-determined [seeking contact with cosmic spirit]

5 Will [linking intention therewith]

6 Be done [determined affirmation of acceptance]

7 Amen [confirmation and completion]

Once this might have been thought of as a total sur-render of wicked human will to an enormously superior spirit called GOD, who meant to do what He or It wanted regardless of how humans felt. Naughty little man with dreadful sensations of guilt and failure meekly handing over the conduct of his life to great big brother God, who was good enough to take charge and get man out of the mess he had fallen into through his own fault. A pretty picture if an inaccurate one. What we actually do is ac-knowledge our fallibility and limitations on merely hu-man levels of living, and therefore have enough com-mon sense to move the intentional direction of our lives back into those deeper regions of our beings which reach a life-level we consider divine because of the difference between its nature and that of our ordinary personal pro-jections as people of this planet. We are not abandoning the control of our lives to anyone else except our *selves* in a far greater spiritual sense. It all depends upon which level of life we make our decisions from. The difference between *Man* and *God* may be one of degrees, but the relationship possible is one of realisation.

Now what happens in the case of those who resolutely refuse to rise upon the Tree of Life and insist on conducting their affairs according to the Tree of Evil? If this were purely a matter which affected their own lives and none others, it would not be of very great cosmic con- sequence. They would only exhaust each other's re-sources into extinction and also extinguish themselves if they continued on the same course. Other emanations of self would emerge from the eternal entity in their places, and so cosmos would continue. As we know to our cost, however, intentional evils have such a wide- spread effect at these earth-levels that almost everyone alive here is affected to some degree. It might be a sensible idea to study the Tree of Evil somewhat in detail and see just how real "baddies" build up their "invisible empire of evil". It is always wise to know one's enemy, whether this is another individual or, worst of all, part of oneself.

Chapter Six

The Tree-Plan of Imperfection

W hy does any entity, human or otherwise, persist in a policy of intentional evil? What does he get out of it? What can anyone obtain from Evil which could not be gained in much better ways from good, or better still, a state of poise between the principles?

Why indeed this peculiar preference for ill rather than anything else? There is only one answer. To subsidize a chosen self-state at an artificially inferior individuation level for the sake of egoic assertion contra to cosmic laws of life. In other words, "I'll do as I like in defiance of all else and be damned to any consequences". Such a direction *cannot* come from a supreme source of being in any sense. It can only originate with a lesser "break- away" point from our initiating intentions where our legendary "fall" began as we acquired enough autonomy to conduct our life-courses volitionally at progressively lower levels.

It would be equally true, of course, to say that we "fell" into good as well as evil ways of living. A conventionally "good" person is motivated by similar self-determining intentions to a "bad" one. They, too, want to

132

individuate as sort of artificially conceived egos in a happy "heaven- state" of their own making. They are not so concerned in becoming what divinity intends, so much as with divinity being what they expect or demand. Like the "baddies", they are content to stop short of total truth and impose their conceptions of well-being impartially among all other lives regardless of any acceptance factor. "Goodies" are convinced that if only the whole of life were universally good, all would be unbelievably wonderful for everyone, especially themselves. "Baddies" are equally certain that if only living might be made evil enough, nothing could be finer for them than their undisputed domination of a state so chaotic that cosmos could scarcely negate everything without eliminating its own intentions. We may be reminded here of the parable about the tares and grain harvest, or the analogy of a condition which could not be cured by intervention except by killing the patient.

Apart from all this, it is well to consider sometimes that we humans are scarcely the only intelligent types of entity in the whole of existence. The deeper our lives link up with what to us are "inner dimensions", the closer do we contact species of being whose condition in relation to ours is relatively that of pure energy which is commonly affected by a connected consciousness and intention. Depending upon which side of our natures these appeared to influence most, so were they once broadly classified as "angels" or "devils". Sometimes just as good or bad angels. They, like us, seemed to favour one or other of the opposites, or else rise sheerly between both toward spiritual heights we can only conceive through negative inference. All mythologies agree that such spiritual entities and ourselves share at least some common interests in spheres of living which extend far beyond the limits of this particular planet. Our ultimate destiny and theirs is connected by life-links which go back to the same origin and ultimation. Therefore having mutual causes to serve, some kind of symbiosis should prove possible between such variant entities for their particular purposes.

This is actually the reputed difference between black and white magic, the former consisting of intentional inner workings by ill-willed humans in collusion with equivalent non-human entities, while white magic is an inner activity shared by beneficent beings on both sides of their dimensional dividing line. Few magical traditions reveal much of "sacro-magic", or the "sacred- secret" spiritual methods transcending all other branches of the art, because it "centripoises" directly between divinity and those employing it. Only very truly trained and advanced adepts dare invoke its aid to any marked degree. Lesser initiates prudently handle its reflective representations which are nevertheless sufficiently potent for most requirements of human inner necessities.

It is an interesting point to note that whereas mankind is credited with ability to commit good or evil at will, his spiritual colleagues are believed to have bound themselves up with one extremity or the other for the rest of existence. While there is no real inner evidence that any purely spiritual entity is irrevocably cast into good or evil courses beyond all possibilities of alteration, it would seem that these tend to either direction much more definitely than we do. Since their inner constant is very greatly more stable than ours, their rate of change is naturally over a far wider and farther ranged arc than humans are accustomed to. So it would seem to us that they are permanently committed to courses of conduct because these extend considerably longer than human lifetimes or eras.

The old idea that humans are influenced to good deeds by one type of spiritual agency or to evil activities by others has a basis of truth, but only insofar as we acquiesce in either direction. Decisive responsibility always rests with those concerned to whatever degree they have achieved individuation. Man in the mass, though, is usually too spiritually inert for much movement either way, which is taken advantage of by both opponents operating inner inclinations. The aim of either "side" is the same, namely to utilize life-energy made available through human activities on all levels for their specific purposes. Since their "ways of life" for establishing identity are even more oppositionally divergent than ours, they need supplies of energy from every convenient immediate source, and we happen to be comparatively accessible as more or less willing donors of this valued commodity. Conversely, we obtain exchanges of energy in terms of stimuli along sub- conscious levels which are fed back into our lives or converted into consciousness one way or another, and so the cyclic changes continue.

Although these inter-dimensional dealings are conducted on living-levels usually well away from areas of normal awareness, they do have very considerable effect upon human destiny. Not that we should suppose for one instant mankind is no more than so many pawns to be pushed around the cheque red board of fate by opposing powers of good and evil. We are here to make our own ways in life towards ultimate entity or extinctions, and though we may be helped or hindered to either event, it depends entirely on our individual and collective selves what will become of us. The likelihood is that we should reach the same cosmic conclusions whether or not any other spiritual entities were closely concerned with us. We are quite capable of good or evil on our own accounts, but our linkage with inner categories of consciousness can have effects of acceleration, retardation, or otherwise alter details of progress for better or worse in our living-patterns as these tend toward total truth. Therefore it is worth our while to learn something about how this happens.

The plain motive of dedicated evil-intenders is continuance in the sub-self state which satisfies them through their chosen systems for maintaining egoic conditions mostly at the expense of other beings. A prime need of evil is consumable fuel in the form of usable energy obtained by any means at all from the most convenient source of supply. Hence the symbol of "hell-fire", or prodigally wasted combustion for wicked purposes associated with evil. Cut off those supplies, and evil would be a self-consuming principle reducing to very small proportions of our life-plan indeed. It is a pity that we humans offer such a ready-made fund of force so freely to intenders of evil both human and otherwise. We make it so easy for our forces to be stolen and misapplied against our best interests. Most of the time we just give our energies away quite casually and carelessly. At the rate we are allowing our inner energies to be misappropriated at present, an "empire of evil" could keep itself amply supplied by humanity till at least the end of this earth.

This does not mean we are bad people in ourselves or intend any particular evil. It is just that we are steadily becoming accustomed to exploitation of our energies partly because of clouding inner consciousness, and also due to the extremely clever and intelligent ways these intrusions into our inner areas are being made. Old- fashioned brutal and agonizing methods of applying evil are rapidly being superseded by far superior schemes whereby the worst motivations successfully masquerade as being all meant for our social or humanitarian welfare. So long as we do not actually feel hurt or injured by these insidious demands, we tend to suppose them harmless or perhaps profitable. If they have the side-effects of making us feel important or successful in maybe minor areas which appear artificially large, we are likely to welcome their attentions as they drain away more and more of our resources into carefully constructed channels leading in opposite directions from what should be our finest and foremost aims of life. Even methods of evil evolve, and it is proving more practical to purchase requirements from unresisting humans than force these out of them by extravagant violence. Docile submissive slaves are always better bargains than resentful and rebellious ones. The surest way of selling evil is to see that buyers enjoy it.

We humans do tend to have very old-fashioned ideas about good and evil. It is as though we needed some focal distance between us and some objective instances before we recognize what we are looking for. We can see it clearly in our past, and even guess it for our future, but as it comes closer and closer to our "now-point" of life, we do not seem able to focus our consciousness finely enough to perceive anything very sharply, if indeed at all. Looking back on evil, it stands out with diabolical definition which cannot be missed by the dimmest viewer. The cruelties, oppressions, sufferings, betrayals and sheer viciousness of man to fellow men are simply beyond question as actualities. How far intelligent inner entities were also involved in these is purely a matter of assumption. The same might conversely be said in the case of good. The point is that we are inclined to associate evil or good with objective instances from our past and use these to estimate or compute our present conditions. This means we are usually quite inaccurate in our current consciousness concerning these important issues, and there is a definite gap, so to speak, between our appreciation of spiritual self-situations and the inner actualities associated with them. It is into that normally unguarded inner area that interference influences may be implanted by those who intend to divert our attentions in whatever directions suit their purposes best. Whether or not we accept or act upon them, however, is another matter.

For these reasons alone, it is well to take very close looks at contemporary forms of evil, being as careful as we can not to confuse forms with forces. There is little point trying to sort out incidents, trends, events and other observable phenomena into classifications of good or evil. That would only lead to greater confusion than ever. The only reasonable guiding rule for recognizing evil as a principle is to look for whatever seem intentionally likely to alienate our self-sense of individuation towards our ultimate identity. This was once described as being a deliberate attempt to interfere between Man and his instinctive growing toward God. That is the real root of evil, whether emanating from other entities or arising of our own accord in ourselves. It may be present in every possible or imaginable form in creation, which could also be equally effective for good. We should always look for intentionally directed forces behind forms, however well these can be concealed from carelessly investigating consciousness.

The Tree-Plan of Imperfection

Figure 2

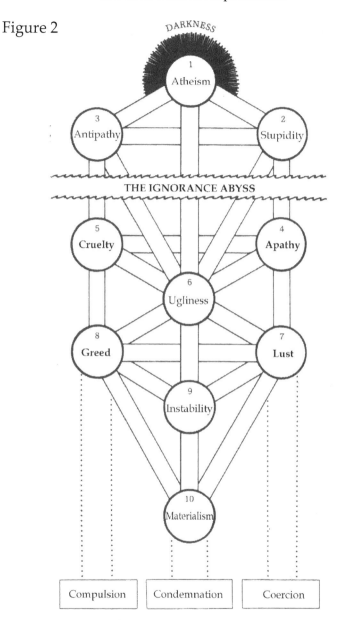

Now we may as well take notice of the Tree of Evil (see Figure 2) which portrays the general plan of intentional promoters of evil per se, and the overall network in which we are caught up during our self-struggles in search of our ultimate entity. If we consider it briefly point by point as it reaches away from our common earth-level of consciousness, we should learn quite a lot about how it affects our chances of eventually becoming individuants in a life beyond any bodily boundaries.

About the first point of interest is the pillar lay-out which shows clearly enough that the factors of *compulsion* and *coercion* drive us along a centre-course of *condemnation* towards eventual extinction. It does not follow that these are only applied to us from outside, as it were. We can apply them to ourselves, or worse still, attempt inflicting them on others. The difficulty here, of course, is one of definition. Compulsion consists in illegal use of force or threats to achieve aims, but what exactly constitutes the illegality? At what point, for instance, would the same force become justified if otherwise applied, and when might a threat conceivably become a warning? Also where does a corruptly coercive scheme turn into a straightforward incentive offer or permissible benefit? There has to be a dividing line somewhere, and this must undoubtedly depend upon motivation.

About the only fair description possible concerning coercion and compulsion where this applies in a spiritual sense is the intentional application of energies calculated or believed to interfere adversely with the natural processes of perfection inherent in individuals, species, or other kinds of existing entities. Otherwise, directed action or arrangement which in some way prevents or retards our evolution toward increasingly perfect states of spiritual being. This may sound a very "blanket" sort of definition, but it has to cover a vast field of living. It bases on the assumption that we are imperfect beings seeking our supreme state of life. If we were able to establish direct links with the cosmic condition and follow those lines faithfully, we should ultimately arrive at such an apex and "zero out" into a state of "perfection". In the case of mankind at least, this seldom, if ever, happens with any consistency because of the diversionary possibilities which interfere with the process. Where these act against our highest interests in life, they broadly vary between extremities classified as *coercion* on the "pleasure" side of our self-scales, and *compulsion* on the "pain" side. Shuttled from one to the other of these, the middle course is one of *condemnation* to continue in that unsatisfactory state until released by "redemption" or extinction. In the case of "redemption", we would have to convert the Tree of Evil energies into those of the Tree of Life.

Coercive and compulsive factors are usually applied to living beings by themselves or others for purposes of profit in some way, however far-fetched this might seem. The malicious motivation lies with the injustice and disregard of what might be called common cosmic law involved. Maybe a religious person might think of this as dishonesty in defiance of divinity. In this world it is certainly exploitation of others (or oneself) in order to satisfy very inferior substitutes for self on lesser levels of living. However one considers this matter, it becomes increasingly clearer why these unpleasant characteristics form the lateral extremities of evil on its tree. Even in terms of this world, an extremity of compulsion would wipe out most of us in the most horrible manner, and an extremity of coercion would enslave us utterly in a futile and foolish state of complacency holding no hope of higher spiritual living standards. Both terrible alternatives. Let us take care that excessive fear of the one does not drive us too far over to the other.

Now for study purposes, let us assume that a deliberate campaign of evil is actually mounted not so much specifically against humanity, as involving us with it because we are, so to speak, "in the field of operations". What might we expect to encounter at this earth-level of life, which would be aimed against our ever evolving any higher? On the Tree of Evil scheme this reads out as *materialism*.

Right away this signifies a refusal to recognize any kind of living away from this world, or indeed taking the least interest in supramundane affairs. All forms of religion, mysticism, magic, or the slightest hints of spiritual states must be resolutely rejected. Being begins with physical birth and terminates with death. Provided we stay within whatever bounds have been laid out by our "people-planners" our brief lives here may not be too bad. After all, we are only animals to be eaten up by earth when we are surplus on her surface. And so forth and so forth. The principle of all this is to divert us away from inherent divinity at all costs, whether by distracting attention, screening and obscuring viewpoints, or any other likely tactic.

People who are prepared to accept materialism as a way of living offer no opposition to intended evil or very much opportunity for intended good. So long as they willingly remain with their noses firmly glued to the ground their eyes are unlikely to discover any stars. They are no threat to evildoers at all. True, they may, and often do, draw distinct lines at physical or observable ills that might be traced to chemical and allied causes, but they will cheerfully allow all kinds of much more subtle and spiritually dangerous contaminants of consciousness first because they do not believe these have any reality, and then because they suppose that whatever will not respond to physical treatment can scarcely be much of a menace in a totally material world.

The more humans who can be held as relatively happy captives of entirely earthbound environments, the greater opportunities occur for dedicated evildoers to operate on levels rather above the heads of those who refuse to uplift themselves beyond bodily bounds. In addition, if evil is intelligently presented as socially or economically expedient, it is incredible what materialists will not only accept, but actively insist upon. Perhaps the worst evil possible among materialists is to become convinced there is no such principle as evil at all. It has been said that the devil being the "father of lies", his greatest deception has been to disguise himself from humanity altogether.

At all events, materialism might positively be marked up as a high major score for the "baddies" of life, whether incarnate or not. At a stroke, it reduces any serious opposition to their intentions right down to minimum. It may not provide overwhelming possibilities of profit, but it does at least afford a definite workable basis in this world for whatever worst might be coming to it. By clever use of the powerful coercion-compulsion per- suaders to discourage man from seeing his divine spiritual heritage, humanity may remain condemned to the eventual extinction of all who refuse to rise above their material marks.

Suppose, though, that a large number of people do try at some period of their lives to reach beyond their bodily limits and find something better to exist for? What then? The next evil of instability deals with very many of those daring to raise their noses inquiringly from the dust in search of cleaner areas of consciousness. In that sphere all the doubts, hesitations and everything to upset mental and spiritual balance is encountered. Here we find con- fusion, weakness, distortion of vision, insanities and all the rest of associated factors calculated to push people away from their proper inner paths as far as possible. This is the sphere where drug addicts, fanatics and other assorted unstables fall back into the morass they made for themselves out of the mess they encounter. This is where one meets the vague and pointless wanderers who flit from one possibility to another all through their lives until they muddle all these up into thought-tangles around themselves they rarely seem to get out of. That is symbolised by the thorn-bush usually linked with lunar levels.

Inner instability is capable of holding souls back for many incarnatory experiences. Until we learn how to stand steadily on something with spiritual solidity, we shall never get anywhere making much sense. The secret of this, of course, is to take almost any spiritual system, however shaky it seems, and believe in it until it becomes solid enough to climb on for the first few steps, anyway, up the inner ladder of light. That is something which doubtful ditherers seldom discover for quite a long time. Many, indeed, shop around a lot of different-seeming spiritual possibilities, shy away from the fallibilities they find in them all, and then fall back again into materialism because it seems a better bet or a more substantial half loaf.

With the sphere of *instability* it is possible to break human beings into sheep-like creatures running hither and thither around every immediate area of inner inquiry until they become too exhausted or indifferent to care much what happens to them. An expert of evil knows perfectly well that once faith in life is shaken to its foundations the rest becomes a pushover – in his favour. From his standpoint people must not be allowed to reach a stable faith in their own purpose or spiritual status. So everything possible should be done to weaken or obviate this. Their beliefs or attempts to believe in anything beyond points permitted by evil-intenders for their own convenience have to be ruthlessly or cunningly shattered. By hook or by crook all has to be kept in states of apparent change and uncertainty, so that definite beliefs become almost impossible. The more contrived confusion the better for the "baddie", who stirs it around while knowing quite well what it is for and how much profit to expect in due course. If there is a maliciously motivated entity considering itself the devil, its smoke-screens probably pay better dividends than its fiercest flames.

Despite all attempts to confuse, bewilder and make people lose faith in themselves, which is the worst of losses in life, people do manage to struggle through somehow and get hold of something to live for which they consider sound, however unsatisfactory it might be otherwise. The next evil on the list to prevent their possibilities of perfection is plain old-fashioned *greed*. This one is too obvious and well known to call for any comments. It was once said the love of money was the root of all evil, but this specific has a back base of sheer greed. Once people fall into the "grab-gimme" trap they usually stay there a long time. Money grubbing is only greed at material levels. Real greed extends a lot further inward than just that. Greed for glory, admiration, anything at all. Greed always associates with unearned misappropriations. A really greedy individual or concern is not interested in entitlements or fair returns, but with unwarranted acquisition of whatever is wanted merely for the sake of having it. One might call this an artificial expansion of ego by attempting to stuff the self full of availables with small regard as to consequence. Greed is almost, if not quite, synonymous with senselessness, and its appeal is mainly for the lower categories of evil- workers.

Well-hooked greed-grubbers may be relied on to pig happily away for age after age unless something causes them to seek higher hunting grounds. Just in case they might have better objectives in mind, the next evil of lust awaits them with metaphorically open arms. Though *lust* and *greed* have a great deal in common they are not identical twins. Lust is often linked with sexual sensuality, but that is only one of its aspects. Lust is even less sensate than greed, blindly demanding what it wants, utterly careless of what happens to whom so long as objectives are gained. Genuine lust has not the least consideration for the feelings of others while it endeavours to satisfy its own cravings. Where even greed might stop somewhat short for fear of reprisals, lust would leap into a funeral pyre for the sake of pyrrhic victory. It will destroy what belongs to others which it cannot snatch for itself. Lust is a very dangerous demon indeed.

Those supposing themselves superior to the lures of lust might do well to suppose again. Lust is primarily a profanation of love and a degradation of loveliness to the lowest possible level. It smears and contaminates all affectionate feelings, sneers at sentiments, destroys delicacy and generally reduces all human attempts at refinement or artistry to the least common denominators. Lust has nothing to do with "earthiness" or even "honest vulgarity". There is no humour at all in lust, only jeering at the expense of the unsuccessful. It is possible to lust in so many ways other than sexual. Lust for money is different from greed for it, being more obsessional and incessant. Greed can become temporarily choked by over-consumption and slack off with surfeiting, but lust may continue unchecked through all its outpaced achievements. It is impossible to satisfy lust, only increase it with each offering of appeasement made. It is insatiable. Nothing but real love can extinguish it.

Bouncing between lust and greed, humans can be held captive on low life-levels a very great while. They are such popular evils, especially during this era that we tend to be over-tolerant of them to almost disastrous degrees. We take it for granted that humans more or less have to be greedy and lusty, as though this were an obligation on everyone and any other kind of conduct was abnormal. Not that lust should ever be mistaken for sexual dealings among people. Lust is actually anti-sexual, since it blinds its victims to everything about sex except the sheer physicality involved, plus the semblance of power over partners thereto. There is always an element of conquering where lust is concerned, with entire indifference to injury or suffering inflicted. Lust is not so much cruel as careless.

If any part of someone's self-hood should happen to break the greed-lust barrier, an evil sphere entitled *ugliness* awaits entry. By ugliness we are to understand in harmony, unbalance, distortion, inaccuracy and allied meanings. For instance, this would signify that untruth could be classified as ugly, so might any form of deliberate misrepresentation or vilification. It could be more widely defined as blasphemy against beauty. Any factor which might be taken to make life seem horrible, miserable, wretched and repulsive. That is ugliness in its worst possible sense. It implies denial or denigration of divinity in man or otherwise, and could be another form of materialism in more subtle shape.

We do not have to look far in this world before we encounter ugliness in all directions, but most of it has been man-made. In nature, it is very rare to find ugliness, while in human affairs it is everywhere. Its roots lie in our refusal to recognize or live by the rules of cosmic harmony which should balance our beings into states of perfect poise. This reflects all around us at every level. It could be seen in the horrible conditions of squalor and disease prevalent in the last century due to greed for gain, lust for power and privilege, instability of ideas, and materialistic standpoints. It can be seen today in "rat- race" greeds and lusts, with the same instabilities and materialities translated into twentieth-century terms. We have ugly outlooks at life, we accept ugly interpretation of it in art and literature, and are deafened by ugly sounds derived from ugly machinery. It is an interesting side-issue that whereas in the last century our poor were dirty, smelly, ugly and dressed in shabby rags purely because they could afford nothing better, nowadays their descendants pay big prices for dirty looking and ugly clothing, unkempt and hideous wigs, and surround themselves with artificial dirt and disorder which costs a good deal to upkeep. The price of ugliness as a marketable commodity has gone up like everything else.

Once upon a time there was a saying "'as ugly as sin", because sin was supposed to separate us from divinity. It is almost as though we use ugliness quite deliberately to disguise from ourselves the beauty we refuse to face. Worse still, we will not even recognize ugliness as such. It is not the ugliness which horrifies, appals, revolts, or upsets us which is really dangerous, because that would mean we should reject it uncompromisingly and seek something better straight away. The deadly type of ugliness is that which we accept on purpose to screen our somewhat hideous states of unsatisfactory self-hood from the blessed beauty which would show this up only too clearly. Rather like painting windows with grimy designs to hide the shoddy and depressing stock inside. One might say we surround ourselves with muck so that our own dirty messes don't seem as bad as they are. That is what ugliness means. Making the worst of ourselves on purpose to avoid perfection.

Just in case there are those who refuse to be caught forever by ugliness and seek some alternative, the evil of *cruelty* makes its claims. Cruelty is something we recognise so easily as a physical activity, yet find so hard to identify in its finer but no less dangerous forms. It is essentially an intentional misuse of power by a strong entity toward a weaker one on the same plane of action. For instance, a helpless cripple could scarcely be physically cruel to a strong and healthy person, yet could very well be diabolically cruel mentally to the same person if he were intellectually vulnerable. Cruelty is only possible as a calculated discharge of destructive energy directed at feebler creatures unlikely to retaliate effectively. Thus cruelty automatically implies cowardice as well.

The motivation of cruelty is commonly again the artificial ego-enlargement resultant from its practice. It makes the little boy feel bigger when he kicks his baby brother. If we can make others frightened of us we seem larger by comparison to their shrinking. That is the secret of cruelty. A false sense of boost because of aggressive action which appears to avoid injurious reprisals. To hurt and kill some helpless and defenceless creature makes cruel people feel enormously powerful by contrast. They may even delude themselves for an instant that they are acting like gods. Taking their pathetic little share of life-energy, they are willing to expend this on damaging the lives of weaker beings for the sake of supposing them-selves more powerful than they truly are. None cry louder than such cowardly criminals when justified retribution rebounds on them. Nobody hates being hurt more than those who hurt with hate.

We need not always look for evident violence in order to recognise cruelty. It is possible to be extremely cruel in the "nicest and sweetest" ways. Staging little scenes deliber-ately to humiliate and hurt someone's feelings while re-maining self-righteously on the side of conventional virtue meanwhile. With the aid of a little intelligence people can contrive all sorts of cruelties yet them- selves keep in the clear so far as rule-books apply. Attendants in mental hos-pitals, for instance, have ample opportunity on these lines. So has anyone in charge of children, animals, or whoever is unable to hit back where it hurts most. Let those who think they could not be cruel examine what conscience they have within their own life-frameworks. If we are still in human bodies then we are yet capable of cruelty in some degree or another. It is well to see this and convert our energies otherwise as we can.

It should not be forgotten we can be most cruel of all to ourselves. The "sado-masochist" syndrome is a very sad one. Those who torture one level of themselves at the instigation of another get caught up into some of the most vicious circles humans can create. Our history books are crammed with instances of horror due to this one fiendish propensity. So much of it may be disguised as pseudo-sanctity or religious righteousness. We do enjoy hiding our nastiest natures behind the holiest seeming hypocrisy, making others suffer for what we inflict on our own egos.

To some extent cruelty is a self-limiting characteristic of evil because in the end people either sicken of it or get so heavily hammered by well-deserved retribution that they quieten down out of sheer fright. Though the propensity for cruelty may remain dormant, it is not likely to leave humans entirely until they learn how to feel much greater still by means of disciplined self-authority applied with justice. Those who might imagine they have become free from evil once they leave cruelty behind for a while have another thing coming to them. Evil again awaits them with the vapid smile of *apathy*.

It is interesting to observe that as we go up the Tree, evil appears to "tart itself up" accordingly. The higher we climb, the more elegant or stylish evil seems. Here is a really harmless looking evil to keep humans quiet in the neatest way. Apathy. Unfeelingness." Lack of interest. Not selective neutrality or "centring out", be it carefully noted, but sheer deliberate; refusal to accept whatever responsibility is due from all living beings on behalf of others. Apathy, like cruelty, is a strong person's failing toward feebler creatures. The withholding of aid or comfort which could be of help to others in leading their lives lightward. It implies a callous indifference towards the needs of others who are seeking linkage with divine life. Apathy carefully ignores all calls for aid of whatever kind from fellow-beings attempting to raise themselves closer to divinity. It says tac-itly: "Even if I'm not holding you down I shan't offer you the least assistance in getting up".

What is important here is recognition of apathy on this account. We have no warrant at all to interfere offi-ciously in the lives of others, forcing our ideas down their throats "for their own good". Zealous and importunate missionising is only another form of spiritual coercion. Compulsion and coercion into conformity with codes im-posed for the convenience of the compellers usually stem from evil intentions. There is only one right way to rise upon the Tree of Life - by one's own efforts directed by inner intentions originating from a supreme self- source. Others can help this process by supplying the necessary extra energies as may best be needed. They can hinder by withholding or confusing these. Apathy is the former alternative.

Apathy is not to be confused with careful non- interven-tion in human affairs best left to work themselves out, or in-action due to respect for principles of privacy where competence in others is taken for granted. It is just lack of willingness to help life toward its highest objectives in oth-ers – or oneself. Indifference concerning one's own spiri-tual welfare is apathy of the worst kind. Those who are apathetic about their own inner conditions are not likely to care much about anyone else's. Inability should never be mistaken for apathy either. Apathy always stems from a refusal to employ capability in the cause of cosmos, thereby blocking the process of perfection in those concerned.

Human heads can be hidden in the comfortable clouds of apathy for many lifetimes. It is so easy to look down upon inferiors, supposing oneself at the top of the Tree because there seems nothing but obscurity above. If any feel brave enough to try penetrating that problem, the *abyss of ignorance* opens out to engulf them.

Ignorance is probably the worst evil on the whole Tree. In practice, of course, it applies everywhere, but it is shown theoretically in this position as separating man from the principles of understanding, wisdom, awareness of highest purpose and, lastly, eternal light. In other words, it cuts us off from all that is really worth existing for. Like the other evils, *ignorance* is a deliberate condition. The word means what it says: wilful refusal to learn. It was once said that all humans make the same mistakes, but those who are wise learn from them, while those who are foolish will not. That is real ignorance.

Why would anyone prefer ignorance to other options? The old, old reason again-artificial egoic status. Here this works two ways. If we can prevent others from learning as much as ourselves we can hold them at a disadvantage, and by refusing to recognize anything which might make us seem smaller than our own self-estimations we feel big by contrast. On the principle of "in a kingdom of idiots a fool is wise". Whether we accept ignorance in ourselves from the worst of motives, or encourage it in others to their detriment, it remains what it is, an evil which divides our entire Tree of Life against the best interests of us all.

Bearing in mind the nature of ignorance, we should realise it cannot be countered by mere information, instruction, or so-called education. Well-educated and informed people may yet choose to adopt a course of ignorance for covering their particular purposes. The old truism of none being so blind as those who will not see illustrates the evil of ignorance quite accurately. In the

Tree of Life, this ignorance gap is crossed safely only by experience directed accurately at our highest possibilities or apex of awareness. With the Tree of Evil it is either not crossed at all, or for those relatively few intrepid individuals gaining uncertain footholds on its other side, the next evil of *antipathy* greets them gloomily. Antipathy, or anti-feeling, is a sort of "Let's hate it first, then see if we can bear it later", affair. It is not the same as prejudice or pre-judgment at all, because this means judging before all the essentials are fully realized. Antipathy is an auto- matic refusal to examine any essential whatever. Our old acquaintance ego status comes in again, of course. Antipathy isolates, and the objective here is isolation of ego as a substitute for identification of self. Instead of individuating out into supreme selfhood, antipathetic isolationists attempt to set up a synthetic sort of ego at this point by surrounding themselves with a ring of repulsion for all else.

Apart from *antipathy* toward others, it exists inside oneself as a firm rejection of all self-ability to understand meanings in life and perceive its ultimate purpose. To some extent antipathy for others may be due to past sad experiences or memories of unhappy relations with fellow mortals. That can be overcome or wear off normally. When antipathy is based on refusal to recognise one's own connections with cosmos it is an enormously serious evil. Being antipathetic to one's real and true self is one of the worst possibilities on the whole Tree. Worse still, it is commonly encountered among more evolved entities. The higher we rise on the Tree of Life, the more deadly become our defects of character on the Tree of Evil.

If antipathy can be fostered or encouraged among whole communities of people they may be more easily controlled by an over-riding authority providing it is possible to contain an entire situation; "divide and rule" has always been a major political maxim. It is one of the oldest tricks in human nature to set people against each other within controllable degrees so that a profit may be gained by the manipulator. Antipathy is one of evil's strongest allies, which is maybe why it has such a high rank on the Tree.

Though it is easy to confuse antipathy with dislike, revulsion, hate, and so forth, the fine distinction is always one of isolation, which again is not to be muddled with insulation. Dislikes and hates are often very close relationships between people or parts of themselves. Insulation implies some necessary protection or preservation. The roots of antipathy lie in refusal of relationship where this could lead to comprehension in a cosmic sense. Supposing that souls and selves ever manage to avoid an excess of antipathy, its complement – stupidity – claims their attention from the opposite corner.

Stupidity is not an inability but a definite denial of wisdom. A stupid person just will not become wise if he or she can possibly avoid this. We should be careful how we accuse people of stupidity when they are perhaps simply slow-witted or unable to comprehend a great deal beyond their very limited mental means. Stupidity has to be intentional. Moreover, it is essentially a refusal to open up the higher faculties or awareness because this might not suit the convenience of consciousness operating on lower levels. A spiritually stupid person may be a very well-informed one, having considerable intellectual capacity and mental scope. In the last analysis, stupidity is sheer determination to resist the awakening of genuine inner wisdom in the self which might direct that self closer to divinity.

Stupidity is not the closing of a mind but of a soul against the awareness of its divine destiny. This may be reflected on lower levels as inhibition of intelligence, but such is the fundamental basis. From a dedicated evil-doer's viewpoint it would be fatal if a majority of people became wise enough to realise their true spiritual structures and inner status. That would deprive the ill-intentioned ones of their power in this and associated inner worlds, reducing them to recognise their very unsatisfactory and inferior states of self-hood, which in turn would break up the little egoic pseudo-selves they had substituted for reality all along. Such a cosmic calamity as having to cope constructively with their own chaos is more than the most earnest evil-doer cares to contemplate. Still, as long as so many mortals seem willing enough to stay stupid, the wicked of our world may flourish at the expense of everyone else.

Stupidity must never be mistaken for simplicity on any account. True wisdom is not mere formal learning or educational qualifications which dissipate with the death of a human brain at the end of its limited lifetime. It is the ability of being aware in the spiritual sense of the term, which means an appreciation of truth in its own self-right. To carry consciousness through all anything IS until its point of unbeing is reached. As humans we can only be really wise in relatively minor degrees, but while we cover even those with a curtain of stupidity we may hardly hope for higher forms of inner freedom. So it is scarcely surprising that all the agencies of evil intending us to remain retarded at this end of existence and serve their ideas of authority rely heavily on the stupidity factor for keeping us down where they mean us to belong. It needs true spiritual simplicity to see through this scheme with one straight line of light.

Whosoever struggles through the spheres of evil on their trees so far, is confronted by the last solid bastion of all: *atheism*. This is not exactly what so many suppose, disbelief in a divine being displaying whatever qualities humans as a whole impute to It or Him. Real *atheism* means refusal to recognize or live by the principles of perfection inherent in oneself. Abrogation of one's own true inner identity, and consequently a deliberate denial of divinity in all else. It is as if anyone said: "I will not identify with the real self which is rightly mine at all. Instead I will break away and stay with the shapes I adopt for maybe many aeons. I know that in the end what I suppose 'myself' will disintegrate altogether and there will be no more of 'me'. However, I am willing to pay the price of extinction in exchange for all the energies of life I may misuse during *my* chosen career through creation". Only a soul or self who is fundamentally aware of the divine entity can be a genuine atheist, since the qualification lies in the intention.

Most of those on earth describing themselves as atheist are nothing of the sort, since if they have not reached any realisation of divinity they cannot possibly reject some- thing so far in advance of their current condition. The most they could claim is refusal to recognise or agree with other people's ideas of divinity or conventional religious outlooks. This is imitation atheism, often leading to sincere searches for spiritual experiences in- dependently of creeds or customs and frequently rewarded with genuine realisations which raise selfhood so much higher up the Tree of Life. So far as evil-doers are concerned, atheism can be a dangerous two-edged sword turning against them if they strike a wrong blow. For that reason it is their last blast in their battle for being.

Practical studies of human history have shown really expert evil-doers that the finest field for fostering the soundest similitudes of atheism among mankind is within the ranks of religion itself. There can barely be any greater deterrent of real human instincts toward individuation than the influence of intelligent agencies disseminating self-destructive doctrine through the mass-medium of evidently authorized religious concerns. Few things in this world are more likely to turn sincere selves from their search for divinity than the behaviour of those claiming exclusive connections there- with. Granted this will probably lead to eventual Individuation in much more direct ways but the confusion and delay involved benefits the "baddies" rather more immediately.

Therefore, if atheism can be "passed down the line" for consumption at ordinary levels of human life, it will work out as so much convenient grist to the "mills of malice". By discouraging or otherwise distracting mankind away from its main mission of seeking its self- salvation, evildoers have bought themselves a longer lease of the life they intend to enjoy just as long as energies are available. Their whole future depends on what we might well call "hi-jacked" or misappropriated supplies of energy from those entitled to apply it otherwise. The more they can compel, coerce, or cajole contributions of "free force" from the rest of creation, the more successfully they will be able to extend their "empire" and exploit fresh opportunities for building up their force-funds of "conscious capital". With sufficient energy behind them they can go on existing and exerting their influence for the rest of what we term "time". That is far too long for any satisfactory spiritual standards.

Beyond atheism what "ultimate evil" exists? After

that point the Tree shows only *darkness* as an antithesis of *light.* This means that whatever it may be lies outside our wildest conception of evil as the least likely to affect our living. Symbolically such a state is "chaos", total disorder, the opposite of cosmic individuation, utter extinction. It carries an implication of our entire ruin in all directions and a degrading devolution until we are "eaten up by evil" altogether and absorbed as a kind of "fuel" for the "powers of darkness". One might say we finish up that way feeding the flames of hell, if not in a literal sense then certainly an end to that effect. In a more modem way we might consider our eventual end with evil as being reduced to fuel for some incredible nuclear reactor providing the powers of darkness with the energy needed to continue their nefarious existence. We can at least feel some security against such a fate in the fact it need never happen to anyone against that individual's true intention.

Those are the workings of the Tree of Evil as far as humanity is concerned mainly in this world and associated states of experience. It is hardly a worse prospect than those we have translated from it into a technology threatening everyone alive. With all the improvements and advances we have made in our ways of living in this world, we are improving and advancing evil at the same time. Whether good is keeping pace could be a matter of cynical speculation, but the probability is in favour. We may find our *new good* just as difficult to identify as the *new look evi1* being created all around us. Let us try and discover what its appearance might present for our judgment.

Chapter Seven

Evil Old and New

It was easy to recognise evil in the bad old days. Everybody knew it went around like a roaring lion seeking what it could devour. People got hurt badly by evil, and the wicked usually stood out like sore thumbs as oppressors, meanies and assorted nasties doing all kinds of horrible things to make this world worse for others but better for them. Of course the devil drove them to this. That was a sound excuse, anyway, and they could conveniently blame the devil for all they did wrong. Why, though, one has to ask, should they have felt need for any excuses or explanations to others? Why not just be evil and have done with it? Why the scapegoat of the devil – unless, of course, they knew quite well in themselves they were doing wrong and had to invent some plausible fiction, hoping to avert the judgment of their own true selves. How many humans try to cover up their own iniquities from *that in them* which wills otherwise? How foolishly tragic it seems, attempting to live a lie in the face of one's own truth. Yet so we do and suppose we get away with it because no immediate action appears out of any empyrean to reprove us.

A few incarnations back we should have said the devil tempted us and so was to blame for our conduct. We knew what the devil looked like because of his pictures in church. He was a goat-like monstrosity with bat wings. The super-baddie who spoiled our chances of heaven

160

and fried us up for ever in hell for his evening's entertainment, television being out of the picture just then. Modern apologists have tried to improve the devil's image somewhat by suggesting that he was the god of an old fertility faith, representing a horned and hoofed herd animal who provided the necessities of meat, leather, cheese, milk, butter and other by-products of vital consumables. His life had to be sacrificed for the welfare of his human herders, so in return they made him into a god-image, etc, etc. Plausibly possible. Very. But accurate? Only partly. Let us see the other side of our goat-god.

Although the goat as an animal has many practical uses, it has one terrible and devastating property. If unchecked, it can destroy a whole area of the earth faster than almost any other creature except man. The process is straightforward enough. As should be well known, the goat eats almost anything of a vegetable nature. It will eat the bark of trees standing up on its hind legs to get at the best bits. In a very short time it has eaten all round the trunk in a circle, and once this happens that tree is doomed. Tree after tree dies off. Given a long, dry, hot period, a forest fire of all this dead wood is almost inevitable, and that catastrophe burns off what may remain of other trees, leaving a wilderness. If sufficient goats survive, they will eat up anything trying to grow later. With the trees gone, rainfall lessens in the area and topsoil begins to blow away and desiccate. The end-effect is an infertile desert incapable of supporting any life worth mentioning, the prime cause of this being goats. That is said to be the story of the Sahara Desert, once reputed as the granary of Africa. Nomadic tribesmen with their goats are believed to have reduced it into its present condition of desolation.

We should easily see how the goat became a symbol of evil. A few stray animals in a matter of days could wreck a whole year's harvest and ruin an entire tribe or settlement of agriculturists. The damage would be irreparable in those days without insurance companies, and people would perish miserably because of the goats' depredations. It may not be easy for us to see this in our times; but our ancestors knew it only too well. Goats were no gods to them, but devils to be feared and dealt with drastically. They had learned how to exorcise this kind of devil. Keep it tied up or confined where it could not harm people's valuable crops. Restrict its movements and control its breeding. Then, and only then, might the creature serve some useful purpose. The secret was to hold it in control always. Nevertheless, its inherent nature was such that it could only symbolise evil to hard-working, industrious, and civilisation conscious humans.

The goat never has been a beneficent god-image, but only one of destruction, malice, over breeding and whatever stands for the downfall of human efforts with nature. What was planted with loving care got devoured with almost contemptuous greed. Even the noises made by goats sound like sneering sniggers. To horrified growers, nothing would look or sound more hellish than the last of their products disappearing down the throats of a horde of chuckling goats. They could well believe these villainous animals had been deliberately sent on such a malicious mission by the "Head-Spirit of Evil" itself, whoever that was. No wonder the goat became so universally accepted as the symbol of evil among all rural communities. It stood for all they hated and feared as a direct opponent of their way of life. The goat is no good old god gone wrong in people's minds. It was a menace from the beginning unless kept under control by very strict methods.

So with the Satan-concept of an anti-life being opposed to human spiritual development in particular. It represented everything in existence which could keep as much of mankind as possible on the lowest of living levels for the longest periods imaginable. Its ultimate hope was to drive a miserable and degraded mankind out of life altogether. Insofar as it might, this spirit of evil sought to hold humanity in states of stupidity, brutality, poverty and backwardness along a line of regression leading to extinction. Wherever some souls managed to fight and struggle their way above these points of inner peril, the "Satan-spirit" suggestively impelled them to look back and misuse their fellow beings for similar reasons, thus becoming willing allies of the satanic process. Their reward for this betrayal was a percentage of profits, payable in currency of this world's coinage.

When the differing cultures of temple sophistication and rural simplicity blended together, their varying concepts of personified evil merged into a satan-goat figure. An uneasy blending, maybe, but it did have meaning for those who arranged it. By personifying all that might go wrong with their lives into suitable symbolic shape, they could at least get some sort of a spiritual grip on their inner situations and deal with these in their own ways. Once they accepted a conventional symbolism for whatever was worst in themselves and life in general, coping with problems arising became a matter of what might be called "metaphysical mathematics". Given a workable set of symbols or figures, any problem can be set up and solved by those having the requisite skill and intentions. If the factor or factors behind all we regard as evil can be summated into a devil-symbol, and those of good into a god-symbol, we might at least attempt to solve the eternal enigma of our existence. The main difficulty is that to achieve this we need to find a position of poise between the two and work from there. This is what mankind either has to find in the relatively near future or face extinction as a species one way or another.

How real is God? As real as all the good in us and extending otherwise incalculably. How real is the Devil? As real as all our evil and extending commensurably to an unknown degree. How real are we? As real as we may rise toward our supreme spiritual selfhood in *perfect peace profound.* When man comes to realize his true cosmic mission and claims his inheritance of inner identity, then life will become, as it should be on all levels for us. Our chiefly immediate danger is that it may take a disaster of world-wide proportions to awaken survivors sufficiently for recognizing their real spiritual situation. If indeed that is avoidable (which some find very difficult to believe hopefully), then we are either averting or accelerating such an event during this present period of our history. It remains to learn which course will win out.

One of our spiritual problems in modern times is lack of satisfactory symbolism for illustrating inner actualities in the light of our expanding experience. Though neither God nor the Devil are dead so far as their functions are concerned, their old-fashioned forms have little or no meaning in contemporary consciousness. The goat has become an agricultural anachronism, and crucifixion means little in an age accustomed to mass-murder. Even a beneficent father-figure gets obscured by state- supplied forms of financial and social welfare. Who would bother praying for blessings available from state- guaranteed funds or other commonplace sources of commodities? Who goes looking for God when earthside economists can organize everything we used to petition the power of life for one way and another in our temples and elsewhere? Everything? Maybe not, but do we realise this sufficiently for the sake of what remains of our souls we have managed to save from supermarket slavery?

The old patterns of good and evil we used to know are opening up and changing into almost incredibly different arrangements of energy in far wider inner dimension. They are altering to virtually staggering degrees. Ultimately our consciousness will cope with this, but the rate of change itself is a bewildering and bothersome experience. So long as we realize that the fundamental principles cannot change, this may afford enough stability for surviving into very transformed conditions of consciousness fairly successfully. We may rest assured that God and the Devil will both be with us still in spirit, but whether *we* shall recognize them for what they are under new names and entirely altered appearances is a moot point. What matters most is, that we begin to appreciate our own relationships with the Inner realities those concepts represent.

However different everything may seem as we reach into what we suppose seems like a "new dispensation" ahead of us, the principles of good and evil will stay constant as they always have. Good being interpreted as whatsoever helps us along our particular paths of life in search of our ultimate identity, and evil is an oppositely directed stream driving us away from that spiritual aim toward eventual extinction. We ourselves will always have the casting vote either way, whether we use this individually or collectively. Nevertheless, it is valuable to gain some working ideas about how the principles are likely to look when redeveloped for future human consumption. We might as well have a few rough notions concerning how to tell goodies from baddies in the world just ahead of us. Then we may choose between them with perhaps a partly clear conscience.

"New look" evil could seem like good to an old-timer accustomed to brutal barbarities and physical cruelties. Those elements would seem absent altogether. In point of fact, they will yet be present in clinical forms. Compulsory operations for "personality problems", and courses of "treatment" to eliminate "anti-social characteristics" will become more and more in evidence. Old-fashioned inquisitors hunting out heresy will be replaced by new-type "examiners" probing people in search of "deviance". No longer tortured and burned, humans will be "treated" and "re-located". The old-style "believe as we do or be damned" alters into "think and behave as we tell you or be deprived". All in the most humane and enlightened method consistent with advancing civilization! No signs of beaten, starving, impoverished or suffering people anywhere. Only com- pliant and unresisting non-entities everywhere, carefully conditioned to fit the framework of "new look" evil forged around them for whatever purpose the "people planners" of that period intend.

Every purchasable resource of this world will be geared up for the most complete captivity of human souls since concentration camps became fashionable. Literally the entire earth is liable to become a prison of its people's souls which they will cheerfully sell in exchange for a percentage in the profits. By that time, ownership of worldwide mass media, and everything likely to influence human thought and behaviour will probably have reached the hands of a single consortium whose policies automatically outline what the rest of mankind is expected to conform with. It is no exaggeration to say that our future living on this planet may depend upon what its new owners decide to layout on the master-tape of a computer designed to determine our destiny here for very many generations.

In case anyone supposes that orthodox religions and creed might prove effective against this "new wave" type of evil, let these ask themselves carefully who is likely to own those establishments, organize them, and pay for their upkeep? Churches are highly profitable concerns, far too useful for wasting in this world. They are ideal collectors of men, money and materials which may be put to any purpose cleverly camouflaged to look like "humanitarianism". Unintelligent evildoers might try abolishing churches or temples altogether, but experts of evil rapidly recognize the possibilities of moving in and taking them over. Devotion pays big dividends whether the stockholders are good or evil.

It is well reputed that the devil can quote scripture for his own purposes. Some might almost believe he wrote much of them himself for the same reasons. Looking at evil worked in the name of Christianity alone arouses a certain amount of cynical suppositions. A competent devil could do far more harm to humanity from churches than with all the so-called "Satanic Temples" and "black lodges" ever invented. Why mess around with theatrical trappings of Satanism at its silliest when so many symbols reaching a far wider section of humanity are so easily pervertible? What devil worthy of the name would need an inverted crucifix to express himself with? All that needs inverting is its meaning. Instead of signifying man's noblest act of sacrifice equating him with his own inherent divinity "after the manner of Melchizadek", the same symbol may stand for human enslavement and defeat on the materialistic cross of death. Far from being banished by a crucifix brandished at him, Satan would calmly take it away and, turning it round, say: "This is how I mean you to be. Bound by your body through matter to the doom you invented yourselves. For my sake, look on this and despair. Call not on your God to save you, for you have murdered Him in your own hearts. He is dead. You alone have said so. In this sign I shall conquer.".

In this world, at any rate, humanity is up against an efficiency of evil such as has not been concentrated here since we evolved into our present forms of living beings. Its chief characteristic will be a completely emotionless absence of feeling and a coldly calculating manipulation of mankind as if by machinery in accordance with a computer-program. Humans may instinctively feel they have been caught up into some strange contrivance of consciousness they cannot understand, do not trust, but have little hope of escaping from, even if they knew where to go. On the other hand, they could not complain greatly of severe ill-usage. Provided they live by required regulations of their society they will be compensated within imposed limits. It will be as if they were "serviced" like the machines they serve in turn, and duly disposed of as they become uneconomical or inefficient.

Perhaps the odd thing will be that no average human

trying to discover who or what is behind all this arrangement is likely to locate anyone in particular. Politicians, public figures and others in view of would-be inquirers will seem to be just parts of a progressive program inclusive of everybody all going the same way. On the surface everything will appear as if a whole society were integrated to its accepted rules. Only the deepest divers may find out what is wrong, and they will scarcely constitute a serious threat to the structure whose deadly weakness they have seen. Attempting to warn or alert others would be a hopeless proposition. Few would even listen and if hearers comprehended the drift and panicked, situations would grow worse very rapidly. The best thing for those recognizing this "new evil" to do is keep such knowledge privately in closest confidential circles, where it may be dealt with discreetly. There will be ways and means to take advantage of it correctly.

Does all this imply that a fundamentally good-natured but otherwise helpless humanity is being sold into satanic slavery by a bunch of upper echelon "baddies" for the sake of bribery on a colossal socio-economic scale? Not at all. There are such big bold "baddies", but they are mainly opportunists cashing in at the deepest ends of an evil, which could not exist among us at all without acquiescence by the majority of mankind. All the top villains do is scoop cream off milk provided by human cows grazing on very green grass. Granted they finance and resell all possible pastures for human herds to fatten their follies on, but if this were not so, hungry humans would change from cattle to ravening predators devouring each other indiscriminately. By buying up the controlling interests in the war business, "big bads" have at least excluded little folk from the field until such time as elimination in a massive degree becomes an economic necessity.

Not that war will cease or conflict die out. While it can be contained or restricted within specific areas and classified as "civil disturbances", "unscheduled social violence", or similar euphemistic disguises, wars will be with us a long while yet before changing again into "conflicts of consciousness". There will be a permitted percentage for war casualties in this world which will be distributed through statistics under a variety of headings concealed by computerism. Here and there all over our world will occur strange outbreaks involving loss of lives, disruption of societies, localised damage and destruction to amenities and, of course, financial re-commitments. Almost none of this arising spontaneously more or less of its own making, but deliberately arranged, planned in advance, catered for and calculated almost to the last decimal of the death-roll. A controlled nuclear explosion of evil, caused for the purpose of supplying energy to the "power-house of hell".

Not that naughty words like "hell" may be permissible in the language of new evil. Nice normal four-letter functional words, yes – but not rude common old-fashioned phrases signifying states of suffering now relegated to laboratories and psycho-social experimental areas (once called battlefields). A fantastic feature of our new look evil is its jargoneering juggling with a once stable verbal symbolism. Experience has shown already that if the most terrible truths or horrifying dangers are wrapped up prettily enough in plastic packs of irrelevant verbiage assembling fresh coinage, people will smilingly accept any brand spiritual of poison put into their ears from somebody else's mouth. Humans are becoming accustomed to this language of chaos, which is actually far more obscene than any plain folk-term for anatomical or sexual detail. Obscenity is that which corrupts or depraves, and surely nothing may be more corrupting or depraving in way of words than those which allow people to accept the sufferings and degradations of others, or their own spiritual subjections, with hypo- critical approval. We profess to condemn Victorians, who smugly surrounded themselves with pious pomposity and absurd pseudo-religious phrase- ology while the rest of their society suffered all sorts of ghastly ill- treatment and injustice. Now we are guilty of putting this very principle into contemporary practice for even worse reasons. What makes us think a megadeath sounds better than a million or more murders?

It is so easy to invent gobbledegookey phoney phrases to make evil more easily accepted. Take, for example, the utterly unreal so-called "generation gap", deliberately contrived by whoever anticipated the biggest profits accruing from an artificial alienation of new generations from older ones. Every new human generation since time began supposes the "last lot" to them must have been a hopeless collection of has-beens. This is quite a normal part of growing up, and equates out fairly evenly in later life. Seldom before, however, if ever to the present extent have youngsters been more cruelly and calculatedly exploited by persuasive "people planners" for such socially and spiritually sordid purposes.

The outrageous audacity of the plan accounts for its semi-success. By means of mass-media and every other brain-bender available the bulk of a whole young generation is persuaded and coerced deliberately to alienate itself from all previous inner traditions symbolized by their parents and predecessors. This immediately creates a sort of vacuum in consciousness which craves to be filled by almost anything convenient. Supplies of shoddy substitutes are, of course, readily available from those who market such stuff to mankind. Youngsters are much more easily manipulated than they would ever care to admit, and once they can be cleverly cut off from their rightful roots they will snatch at almost anything which looks as if it might extend their lives by even a fraction. Worse still, encourage their dependence on what is really rather expensive rubbish, and they will infallibly pay more and more for what can never satisfy their sense of severance from true spiritual values. All this does not only mean mere money dealings, but signifies soul-selling in the blackest of markets. There are worse addictions than drugs waiting to engulf young innocents abroad in this wicked world. The treacherous and altogether artificial "generation gap" engineered by highly efficient evil-doers could yet widen to an abyss holding up human progress for who knows how many millennia.

We speak of "deprived" children these days, meaning those with inadequate supplies of material benefits and "social advantages". Does no one care about the deliberate destruction of spiritual structures which might enable individual human entities to find and follow their own inner ways out of this world? While it is more than right to help the human needs of our fellow mortals on this earth, there should be grave concern felt about all that we and our children are being cunningly deprived of in the realm of vital inner resources we can so ill afford to lose close contact with. If our fundamental life-faiths and basic beliefs are being systematically and scientifically sidetracked away from us, while the traditions we rightly belong with are

172

being subtly sabotaged for the sake of our spiritual disadvantages, it is surely about time we demanded to know just who is trying to deprive us of our holiest heritage for what depraved reasons.

Volumes could, and it is to hope, *will* be filled by comments, criticisms and expositions of our new evil, but how much help this might be is doubtful. What is important is recognition of this new evil as such by ordinary average mankind. Not a sort of sub-conscious tacit acknowledgment with a corollary of indifference, but an actively alert awareness at normal levels of consciousness. What is more important still is that this evil is clearly seen not as something in everyone else or remote threats from an anonymous "they", but as an active energy eating into the heart of observers themselves arising in their own natures. If everyone alive distinctly realized evil in themselves first and neutralized it at that point forthwith, the worst of our problems would be solved straight away. In fact, it is our only solution. There is no use at all supposing that if "they" did anything about something everybody would be the better for it. The right place to cope with evil, old or new style is in oneself.

For all practical purposes, therefore, we may as well personify the sum of evil combined from the consciousness of every entity alive into a satan-concept and call it devil or what we will. In modern symbology the mushroom-blast of the bomb is an obvious sign of evil since it does for us what the goat-demon did for our ancestors – destroys us and reduces our productions to a desert. Conversely, if held in the chains of a power-plant it will supply us with essential energies to serve our way of living. If we compress this again into an anthro- pomorphic presentation, the new look satan could seem like a scientist with colourless eyes and a completely expressionless cast of countenance. Old-time Satan was somewhat of a lusty lad with a fearsome temper. He roared and raged, shrieked, stomped and reviled. Then he would turn round and cajole most charmingly as he solicited for souls. He was all our own faults magnified.

The new *super satan* concept is nothing like this. He has not a shred of anything resembling human faults or feelings about him whatever. He may be imagined as what a "doomsday computer" would look like if it were made in the image of man. The personification of efficient evil. Cold, clean, clinical and fatally final. Maybe the most frightening aspect of this Neo-Satan is that he seems somehow *alien* to our particular conceptual awareness of creation. Our old Satan was, at least part and parcel of *our* universe, related to us by a bond of mutual badness, and so we had that much in common, awkward as it might be to admit. This new Satan appears as if he belonged not so much to us as some inconceivably remote state of uncreation beyond life altogether. Did we invoke him from the abyss by a blast from our bomb? Is he a mutation of our own malice taking an unfamiliar form? Or a sinister "take-over" influence focussed upon us from some science-fictional sphere of anti-life hidden behind our limits of being altogether? Whatever our new Satan may or may not be, he or it is undoubtedly very dangerous indeed, and the sooner we learn how to shackle him the better for us.

The query is bound to come sooner or later concerning what is supposed to be so terrible or disconcerting about the neo-diabolic dispensation likely to eventuate among us. If there is to be a sufficiency of food, clothes, material supplies, amusements, social security, clinical care and other welfare amenities available for humans without much trouble, who cares about anything else? A few minor murders here and there and some localized civil disturbances or population problems demanding military control while politicians plan round the pro- gram, seem a small price to pay for plenty to eat, enjoy and play with. There is only one strict proviso. If it were written as a commandment (which it never will be) it might read: *Thou shalt never be thy Self.* That will be the one absolutely forbidden faculty. There must be no seeking immortal identities or such individualistic behaviour permissible in the domains of any master- minded devil. Plenty of type-patterns will be provided for people to choose from, and they can be pre-set to any, altered as required, or fitted into suit exigencies, as long as they are selected from the stock approved by whatever committee interprets the instructions of its chairman. Any mortal presuming to prefer its own self-design will be penalized with the full rigour of every regulation applicable.

It may seem a very odd thought, but we appear to be reaching for our Garden of Eden myth in reverse, so to speak. The familiar legend there was of a happy humanity free, to do as they liked with only one prohibition – accept responsibility for their own good and evil. This they deliberately chose, and so fell into material shape and a life dependent on biological reproduction in the animal kingdom. Now, after all the evolution we have endured in these conditions we seem likely to face another momentous decision. We may remain as relatively happy humans in this world with our tastes fully catered for, providing we stay content to live and die as advanced animals looking no higher in life than that. Again there is but a single prohibition - seeking individuation with the initial intention which began our beings before we ever emerged from our primal paradisical condition of consciousness. That is the forbidden fruit awaiting our selection or rejection. Whereas the Edenic fruit grew on the Tree of Knowledge, its earthly counterpart grows on the Tree of Life. Last time it was said to be Eve who offered the fatal fruit to Adam. This time it might be a nice gesture for Adam to return the compliment.

A medieval moralist might be forgiven for making up a folktale from this theme. First, there would be God and His garden making everything happy for dear little humans cavorting around in amusing innocence. Play- boy Satan gets jealous of this and thinks "Anything He can do, I can do better". So he suggests to the humans they would have finer value in his supermarket, where bonus trading stamps await all customers not bothered by silly things like conscience. They fall for this literally, and are expelled earthside along with Satan, from whom the humans immediately demand impossibilities as compensation. Altogether, they give Satan a hell of a time for millions of years until he feels like a criminal outcast. Being a smart sort of spirit, however, he eventually organises affairs in this world to suit himself and is just arriving at a position where he can keep some of his rash promises. He has schemes to supervise everything on earth that it makes heaven seem like a slum by contrast. Naturally he expects top cut of this joint. He is just rubbing hands worked into claws from inflicting out-of-date sufferings on humanity in revenge for their ill treatment of him, when a very disconcerting thought hits him where it hurts most – right in his pride.

What happens, he wonders, if instead of staying with his splendid plastic paradise recovered on earth, people might prefer to take up their undoubted option on working their ways inwardly toward individuation and desert him for divinity? All the best people escaping from earth by inner routes he cannot interfere with. That will leave him with nothing but rubbishy remnants fawning around his fetlocks, and even Satan has to draw the line somewhere. The prospect of utterly untalented and inferior specimens of mankind multiplying by myriads and making more and more demands on his demonic abilities frightens even Satan into cold sweats despite his built-in central inferno.

Perhaps what wounds Satan most is the ingratitude of man. Here he has slaved himself nearly to a cinder so that humans may slave for him in return for the keep which seems to satisfy most of their insatiable greeds (there *are* moments when Satan almost feels dissatisfied with his own nature). Now these horrible humans demand more than he could ever offer them with credit extended to its limit. They ask divinity. To become themselves in a true sense. If ever they find out how to lift off his low-level planning and steer starwards toward their own divine destinies, Satan and his sociocracy will be left stranded on a perishing planet while the escapees are whooping it up in a self-state of divine delight.

Satan gets really worried by cosmic competition, so thinks up all sorts of schemes for keeping the bright boys and girls contented by earthside conditions. He offers double - no, treble, quadruple, or any amount of extra trading stamps in return for custom in his establishment. To his joy, most of the hesitant human horde are still bribable. But for how long? That is what bothers him. Can he ever keep pace with those he first instructed in avarice? The inflated prices of souls mounts upward at a rate which alarms Satan dreadfully. Is he capable of coping with the spiritual situation, or had he better let these horn-aching humans go back where they rightly belong? The chances are they will get bored by heaven eventually and be thrown out again. Meanwhile he might have fun watching them climb until they slip or jump back to the positions he plans for them. So long as most of them return to base he does not grudge occasion escapers from orbit their chances. Who knows? Perhaps some day the horrors of humanity might put Satan himself on the return road to primal paradise. After all, like humans, he did start from there until he tried to make more of himself otherwise. Could he just possibly have made the least little error? Banishing the unworthy thought for the time being, Satan attends to his business with increased interest. The world spins on and its inhabitants continue in their courses much as usual Cosmos co-relates itself accordingly. Such is life.

However the tale might be told, its moral comes to the same point. We became, as we are now because of knowing good and evil. We shall become, as we should have been in the first place by knowing the self. The secret of that knowledge is found through growth on the Tree of Life. That is the real story. Locked in every entity are the keys of its own liberation into ultimate light, and not all the darkness existing or Satans old and new that ever will be, can possibly deny the least of beings its birth-right if it decides to claim this in the name of cosmos. True that the life of such a seeker may be made very unpleasant in worlds where the majority vote is otherwise cast. That is only to be expected. Anyone foolhardy enough to proclaim publicly an inner allegiance with an identity no one else believes in is simply asking for trouble they well deserve for senseless lack of discretion. Whoever seeks true spiritual self-hood in this area of life would be well advised to observe the magical maxim of working with knowledge, daring, will and silence.

There is good reason for this discretion. If carefully kept, it effectively prevents any "overlordship of evil" from fully, discovering the strength of its opposition on these levels of life, and that constitutes the one random factor likely to overthrow its most captivating calculations. While there are even a few "loose souls" alive in human arenas who resolutely seek in themselves the truth they believe identifies them with the spirit of life itself, humanity as a whole cannot possibly be condemned to entire extinction. Individuals and uncounted millions of mankind may extinguish themselves forever, yet so long as a "faithful few" carry the light of life in themselves closer toward ultimate unison with *perfect peace profound,* man as a life-species can never become extinct. Those relatively rare beings are the "wise ones" who proceed purposefully through life in this world while acting as agents for far finer spheres of spiritual living in different dimensions of consciousness. Their mission is to provide contact points for forces concerned with human evolution beyond the highest limits possible in mortal manifestation. To that extent they might almost be classified as "secret agents" or operatives on behalf of what others could call divinity by whatever name they chose.

The great value of such souls lies with their unobtrusive presence in a working field of force where evil strives for predominance. While they simply exist here and quietly radiate inner influence impelling other humans in higher directions, the network of evil cannot completely close around its semi-captives. The function of these individuating entities is to keep specific paths open, and act as automatic exchangers of energies derived from divine levels of life. They do not need any physical contact with other humans for this purpose, and would most certainly never reveal anything of their inner construction to inquisitive fellow mortals. Inwardly they have learned how to screen themselves from evilly motivated inquiries up to levels unlikely to be overlooked. None, of course, are infallible, and many a "cover" has been broken or betrayed, yet others always arrive ready as replacements and the cosmic call continues.

So far we have been looking at big brother evil fixing up his take-over bid for worldwide business inclusive of all souls on the staff and employed entities attached. What, if anything, is a presumably good God doing about this meanwhile, and has *He* any acceptable counter- proposals which might interest human share-holders ready to sell stock on such a market? The first and obvious query is why should beneficence of being sell itself at all? In fact, it does not. In no sense does good compete against evil for favours from mankind or any other form of life. Evil may be buyable, but good never. It is utterly without price, and that is the main differentiation between the two principles. If we are expecting to find good in this world starting a cut-price campaign against evil, we should forget such a fantasy forever. That is out of the question altogether. Good never bribes, offers no rewards, and puts no pressures on people to perform their parts in its programme. All it promises are fair and equitable returns for efforts expended on its behalf, not necessarily in commercial currency exchangeable in this world. True good never offers huge profits from minor investments made for the sake of speculation. Indeed it proffers no profits whatever. Nothing but earnings.

There is this to be said, however. Profits accruing from evil are, liable to be lost in a moment, leaving a soul in a state of abject poverty beyond description. "Easy come, easy go", as the saying is. Earnings obtained by good may be infinitely harder to achieve, but will last as long as their holder intends. That does make rather an important difference.

This is why evil seems so predominant in our human world. It proclaims itself all over the place, advertising its presence flamboyantly and flagrantly, being a publicity-seeker everywhere. Strange to say, the actual "top brass" instigators of evil hide behind screen after screen of clever camouflage. No one will admit to being a "super-baddie" or even an enthusiast of evil. It is extraordinary how much evil goes ahead with apparently nobody in the driving seat. In that way evil resembles a tank destroying its target. The crew remain unseen. They would describe themselves as button-pressers. Their machine does the killing and they only obey orders. For all that victims know, there may not be a human crew in the tank at all if it is radio-controlled. Who is responsible for their deaths then? Evil does enjoy excusing and exonerating itself rather than acknowledge responsibility and admit intentions. It also enjoys watching the disasters it instigates from its safest possible shelters, deep inside refuges provided by its willing partisans in human or other shape.

Therefore, whoever may be interested in averting evil from this world had better begin by exorcising it from themselves. That is the correct procedure. A tough proposition truly enough. No legions of good angels are likely to appear with waving lances of light putting terrified troops of demons to flight forever. We may personify good as we will, but it arises in us through our instinctive connections with a consciousness linking us with cosmic life into a single spiritual bond of being. In this world we should note an important difference between manifest good and evil. Whereas evil is constantly trying to advertise itself and attract our attention away from other issues, the onus lies with ourselves entirely to invoke the influence of good into our environment. Good as a *principle* does not inflict itself upon us by compulsion or coercions, but through invitation only. It has no need of this world to express itself with like evil has, nor does it attempt to force itself in unasked. If we want good to enter our earth-lives we have to make room for it in ourselves. It will not come here otherwise. We are the decisive factor whether or not this world happens to be predominantly good or evil. Evil is likely to approach us from all angles, but we have to approach good from one angle only – that which connects us closest with our own true identities. Then we have to learn how to balance and transcend both principles in order to reach truth, but the way there leads reactively from the good side of life first.

We shall not induce good in ourselves by rushing around with all sorts of wild schemes for interfering in other lives or donating vast sums of money to commercial charities. Nor shall we exorcise evil by trying to frighten it away with incense and threats of heavenly retribution. The exorcism of evil and institution of good in any self-area as a preparation for poising the individuant between the principles purposefully pointed toward *perfect peace profound* is a process calling for very exact equation. The only commonsense way to set about it from a magical standpoint is through the Tree-system, taking it stage by stage until it works out as a satisfactory answer. This had better be our next concern in our present study.

Chapter Eight

Dealing with the Devil

For those who prefer personalizations of all powers, the following poem is a rhyming account of what to do with the devil in person. It is a lighthearted approach to the subject with quite serious implications. Its underlying meaning seems to be that it would be very unwise for single individuals to challenge the Prince of Hell without plenty of spiritual support from Heaven. In other words, never pretend to powers beyond abilities or disaster is certain. Sure support from the *forces of light* is available for the asking, but will not interfere unless invited to do so. Here, those Forces are personified as the principal Archangels, while the total *powers of darkness* are summed up into the person of the Devil. A simplistic but serviceable idea. A change of meter here and there marks the alteration of attitude.

Why does the good we mean to do go bad?
What makes the happiness we sought turn sad?
Where do we go all wrong with things we touch?
How is it life can hurt so very much?

Ages ago our ancestors believed
When they felt wrongly treated and aggrieved,

Exorcising the Tree of Evil

That all the evils of existence came
From one appalling source they dared not name.

So they personified this force they feared,
And since it seemed particularly weird
They did not care to call it into mind
Except as something hostile to mankind

Such as *The Devil.* If we need to seek
The origin of this, it comes from Greek.
Diabolus, a lying, slandering one
Is meant when everything is said and done.

In Latin also, which is rather odd
It could be *Deo falsus* or *False God.*
Both definitions meaning much the same
As a description rather than a name.

Then we have *Satan.* That old word of course
Is traceable to a Semitic source,
And signifies *opponent,* one of ill-intent
Who takes advantage of the innocent.

A clever one is *Lucifer.* At sight
It only means *A bearer of the light.*
Yet what bears light? Significance is stark,
What carries Light, can only be – the Dark.

In other words, the troubles of this life,
Its evils, aggravations, and its strife,
Can all be summed to one symbolic head
Personified as everything we dread.

This often is a useful course to take
When wondering what moves mere men may make
Avoiding things we often come across
In life which cause us so much pain and loss.

Dealing with the Devil

Here is the simple answer plain and clear.
If we could focus on a single fear
Inclusive of all else, and concentrate
On that alone, we might avert such fate.

By dissipating energies around
Among the wrongs and worries we have found,
Our forces fritter into uselessness
Instead of channelling through consciousness.

But if we brought those energies to bear
By all the power of which we are aware,
With laser-like intentions on one spot
Of focal evil – we might hit the lot.

So surely this makes most surprising sense
That scarcely calls for special eloquence
In order to convince a lively mind,
We truly need a Devil of some kind.

* * *

What? *Need* a Devil in our day and time?
Are there not enough in human form?
Responsible for every sort of crime
And evil that we think as our norm?

That is quite true of course, but even then
There are deep motivations as a cause
Which could be termed the *Devil-drive* of men
To make us contravene good living laws.

Add such to whatsoever else as well
Is anti-human in this Universe,
And we shall find an Inner state of Hell
As bad as anything we know – and worse.

Exorcising the Tree of Evil

The whys and hows of such a fearsome force
Are matters of opinion and surmise
Somewhat beyond this limited discourse
Of dealing with the Devil in disguise.

Now by *The Devil* should be clearly understood
Our own considered concepts and ideas
Of all that goes against our highest good
And threatens to fulfill our deepest fears.

Let us be certain of this issue here,
Since two points are connected that relate
And we must get them absolutely clear
To see how they affect each others state.

The first is everything in life that thwarts
Our best intentions as evolving souls,
Ill-treats our finest natures and aborts
Our efforts at achieving noble goals.

The second is however we may feel
Or think about such sad perversity
Through terms we use admitting it is real
To help us tackle its adversity.

One is *The Devil* as a living fact
We all experience to some degree,
The other we create as we react
By struggles that we hope will set us free.

Like is a remedy for like they say,
So if we would avoid the very worst
And keep adversities we fear away,
We need the second to combat the first.

Dealing with the Devil

Here is a problem for us right away,
How does a modern Devil look today?
The antique Fiend that caused us so much grief
As a monstrosity, is past belief.

Let us forget those talons horns and wings,
Together with all such outdated things,
And greet the Devil when he now appears
To claim his title as Our *Lord of Fears.*

Is he a mushroom-shaped atomic blast?
Will he cremate humanity at last?
Or does his deadly influence apply
Through factors beyond reach of ear and eye?

Perhaps we all of us have our ideas
Of how the Devil nowadays appears,
If we think up contemporary dreads
And make symbolic pictures in our heads.

Some see the Devil at his old time tricks
Translated into present politics.
Or maybe something else they strongly hate
In social structures, such as church, or state.

To some, the Devil seems most sinister
Disguised as a religious minister.
Or something altogether greedier,
A master-planner of mass media.

A few indeed might very much insist
Their Devil was a sociologist,
Or for that matter "ists" of any kind
Who interfered with what they had in mind.

Exorcising the Tree of Evil

Some find the Devil just a bit too much
In everything they see, hear, smell, or touch.
Yet have they ever thought to look inside
And see if he comes with them for the ride?

Whether in abstract shape or humanoid
Our Devil seems a creature to avoid.
Some people make It altogether neuter
As an Ultimate Doomsday computer.

Then we may choose our Devil how we will
As anything we think intends us ill,
Although it might make some of us feel sick
To see the choice from which to take our pick.

Perhaps it could be called a compromise
To look our Devil straight between the eyes,
And see – a scientist with super brain,
Emotionless, and awesomely insane.

Someone completely icy and remote
In a long, white laboratory coat,
Whose research project would be well defined
As finally frustrating humankind.

*   *   *

When we have got the image of our opposition clear
We next will have to figure out a good position near
For taking up a fighting stance against the Demon shown
And commencing an effective opposition of our own.

Those of us that know about the Seven Archangel scheme
Should discover that we have indeed a really expert team
Of spiritual specialists with weapons which they wield
Called *Crown, Cube, Cord, Sword, Rod* and *Cup,* then finally
a *Shield.*

The Crown belongs to *Metatron* who guides us from on high
The *Cube* unto *Sandalaphon* who keeps up our supply.
The *Cord* connects *Suvuviel,* our link with Verity
The others gather round and help with due celerity.

Raphael ahead of us makes sword play in advance,
Michael upon our right displays his shining *Lance.*
Jivrael behind us pours the contents of his *Cup,*
Auriel at left protects with screening *Shield* held up.

What does this special symbolism really signify?
It shows a way we can proceed and things we ought to try
In order to defend ourselves from spiritual ill
With systematic conduct and at least a little skill.

Above us *Metatron* implies our link with *Life Divine,*
Which should direct the trend of our deliverance-design.
Sandalaphon below us means available supplies
For keeping up the action of this special enterprise.

Raphael distinctly shows how we should be awake
Confronting coming dangers with decisive moves to make
Because a cowardly enemy will rarely risk attack
On anyone who looks prepared and likely to hit back.

Michael means unrightness in the full sense of this term
Which tells us we are justified and keeps us standing firm
With poise and power projected like a *Lance* of *Living Light*
Against all things of *Darkness* in a cause we know is right.

Jivrael would have us act in quite another fashion
Taking up an attitude of merciful compassion
While overcoming Ill with Good, attempting to forgive
Our enemies who are against the way we try to live.

Auriel is caution well combined with common sense
Which causes us to take the best of care with our defence.
Since when a conflict rages round with hatred and
aggression,
The highest valour is no use at all-without discretion.

Suvuviel sums up in us the total Truth we feel
That seems good sense in any life and helps to make it real.
Until we are quite certain we embrace a worthwhile
Cause
Within a cosmic state controlled by spiritual laws.

Then if we mean to face and fight our evil opposition
Such are the principles we need to hold a strong position.
From which to counterbalance whatsoever we shall
meet
And live with some success instead of quite so much
defeat.

We may as well remind ourselves in case we ever falter,
That fundamentals stay the same while their externals alter.
And the best of modern methods we think adequate today,
Will extend into our future in a very different way.

For instance, many years ago, practitioners of Magic,
Being motivated like ourselves by drives that can be
tragic,
Believed they might gain anything if they could but
persuade
The *Devil,* as an Entity, to come and lend them aid.

These operators often thought they summoned up the
Devil
By working in symbolic circles drawn out on the level,
Looking at a smaller circle sketched around the place
Where Satan was invited to appear and show his face.

From such positions, sorcerers invoked Infernal Powers,
And kept their conjurations going for maybe many hours,
Cajoling or commanding fiends in no uncertain fashion
Then if these never answered, roundly cursing them with passion.

What with the herbal drugs they used, or plain old fashioned drink,
And clouds of incense making an hallucinogenic stink
Together with the psychic stress they underwent as well,
They frequently supposed they met some visitors from Hell.

Perhaps today these medieval antics make us smile,
And few would really think such trouble was worthwhile
Yet we must still admit some things in life are fundamental
Especially with Energies so strong and elemental.

If we believe in *Evil* as a principle behind
The purpose, powers and practices of a malicious mind,
Why then the rest is relative, and surely has to be
A matter of convenience, adaption, or degree.

So how we call up Evil is a question of technique,
And maybe modern methods are much easier to seek.
We need not drink and drug and dance, scream blasphemies or rave,
Nor desecrate a church and dig some corpse out of its grave.

Why call up Evil anyway? It is already here.
We only have to think of it to feel it drawing near.
The Devil is not far away, but very close indeed.
A single thought will summon him with quite amazing speed.

191

The Devil is all Evil in each solitary soul
Multiplied by everyone that makes our total Whole.
So each of us should exorcise the devils we have got,
For if enough would do just that, the rest are helped a lot.

To objectify these evils, the simplest way of all
Is make a sort of mental screen on some obliging wall,
Then summon up the worst in you of which you are
aware
And project this as a picture till you see it standing there.

Expel the evil from yourself and get it focalized
Until it can be clearly seen and really recognized.
Do not allow this phantom to alarm or horrify,
But begin an Archangelic counter-action in reply.

One practical procedure of approach that has been
found
Is staying in the centre with your Archangels around,
Then, as it were, rotate them all and consciously direct
Each Archangel to face the Fiend and have its own effect.

For instance make *Raphael* launch an *anti-evil dart,*
Then *Michael* raise his *Rod of Power,* prepared to do his part.
Let *Jivrael* dissolve with *Love* the bitterness of *Hate,*
And *Auriel* hold up his *Shield* against the blows of *Fate.*

Then maybe *Metatron* suggest instructions or advice
While *Sandalaphon* is making up some very good device.
Suvuviel is casting round what Satan cannot stand,
The noose of Total Truth which holds all Cosmos in
command.

So set these out with strategy, or else invent a Call
Which summons in a second some arrangement of them all
The vital thing is feeling that they really do exist
As an answer to the evil you are willing to resist.

What you are doing in effect is to start a state of stress
Which activates its *Archetype* in *Cosmic Consciousness.*
In other words you make yourself become a sort of trigger
For forces in a field of Life considerably bigger.

There are many variations to be made with this idea
And multiple manoeuvres much too long for mention here,
These should come readily enough to anyone that looks
Inside himself for knowledge which is never found in books.

One point must be remembered; when a Devil is attacked
It does not stand there stupidly and let itself get whacked.
Whatever the Archangels do, it will retaliate,
Maybe matching care with cunning, or resisting Love with Hate.

Therefore setting about Satan is a lively enterprise,
And you may as well anticipate some very rude replies.
For after all, the Enemy we tackle in that name
Is something in our natures which is very far from tame.

Unhappily, when our freewill as humankind began
Both Good and ill in us became integral parts of Man,
So in this wicked world of ours, it is quite sad to say
All evil will not vanish till a very distant day.

Then are these thinking-sessions just a silly childish game?
Or some far-fetched foolish fantasy amounting to the same?
Far from it, they are exercises, training up the will
And increasing an ability for dealing well with ill.

What happens in the limits of one human mind and soul
Must necessarily affect a fraction of our Whole,
So every single exercise helps other people too,
And is therefore of good value as a useful thing to do.

Then set this pattern working for the service it can give
Towards reducing evil in these times through which we
live,
For if you care to think of it, no one could ever doubt
That our evidence of evil shows too much of it about.

So there are seven basic points of attitude to learn
In defiance of the Devil, all together or in turn.
Although, of course, the lot amount to only one idea
Of negating evil in us and eliminating fear.

First we must accept there is good *Guidance* from on high
Then we have to seek a *Fount* of spiritual supply
When we get these connected by a line of *Truthful Light,*
The other four are almost bound to come exactly right.

Alertness is essential for all action to commence,
Uprightness proves the standpoint we should take up
in defence.
Compassion is the antidote to venomous intent,
Caution must be always used unto its full extent.

If anyone would change a state of Hell into a Heaven,
They could take great advantage of this *Spiritual Seven,*
And something far too obvious to classify as rumour,
A faculty that once was called *an honest sense of humour.*

Believe this, or believe it not, but Satan cannot bide
The slightest laugh at his expense or injury to pride.
One way of dealing Lucifer a really back-hand stroke
Is treating his attempts to tempt exactly like a joke.

This may not be forthcoming as an easy thing to do,
Unless we can appreciate a Cosmic point of view
Which sees the Satan-Spirit as being Devilishly clever,
But recognises also, that it cannot last forever.

We ourselves have spirits of immortal derivation
Which can uplift our entities past human incarnation.
Contrasting this with Satan, we might feel we could for-
give him
If all he does convinces us that we shall yet outlive him.

While the owner of a "quarrel which is just" may be
thrice-blest,
And whoever "laughs the last" for any reason laughs
the best,
We are likely to lead Satan an unprofitable dance,
When at the end of everything, he does not stand a chance.

That may not seem consoling at this present point of time,
Accustomed as we are to acts of viciousness and crime,
While defeat of all our devils at some day so far ahead
Scarcely seems of great importance if by then we shall be
dead.

For those of us who feel we shall incarnate here again
It matters much that we should work to lessen future pain
And spare ourselves unneeded grief when we return
through birth
By acting now to cancel likely evils on this earth.

The only way of changing conscious evils into good
Is altering our attitudes and thinking as we should
Which calls for endless efforts of intention brought to bear
Against the evils rising from our inner founts of fear.

If we would really exorcise our evils and stand firm,
It might be well to understand the meaning of that term.
There is a double sense to it from ancient Greek, and both
Mean to *Expel,* and "the administration of an oath".

Exorcising the Tree of Evil

An oath of what to whom? In olden days it was supposed
The exorcist commanded devils forth and then imposed
A solemn obligation on them never to come back
Or bother erstwhile victims with a threat of fresh attack.

We can interpret that these days in quite a different light.
The oath of obligation is *our own,* that we will fight
By using modern methods on the demons of today,
And counter them with consciousness until they go away.

Or, best of all, if devils prove offensive and perverse,
The thing to do if possible is - put them in reverse.
So that no matter how they try to work some evil plan
The ultimate results will bring more benefits to Man.

No human on his own is capable of such an act,
And those who think they are had better recognize that fact.
The one sure way for humans to deal safely with their devils
Is by invoking expert aid from somewhat higher levels.

The methods of achieving this are several different kinds,
Religious men call on their Gods, and atheists - their minds.
It really does not matter much, providing consciousness
Is raised and aimed above the range of our inventiveness.

Our Universe is structured so that it will compensate
For every evil in our lives, although at its own rate.
All we can do is work within its range of natural laws
Affecting the relationships between effect and cause.

So dealing with our devils takes a very special skill
Which takes a lot of learning and a vast amount of *Will.*
Yet we must win this conflict, both by strength or stratagem,
For in the end it is a case of either us or them!

The last line tells the whole story. It has always been an "us or them" battle between the opposing Forces that in the end will decide the ultimate fate of humanity in this, or any other world. Previously it has more or less been a question of "win a few lose a few" and carry on struggling, but we have reached the critical turning point.

Whether or not we believe in Devils is actually im- material, so long as we learn to live as if they really existed - which in fact they would if we were able to see them in modern form as concentrations of consciousness, rather than the baleful bogies of our pathetic past. First let us accept that in this world we have to fight against its adversities - or die. That is a law of life which no one can avoid. Then let us *know and recognise* what we are fighting against, and why, and how. In previous wars, posters were prominently displayed showing men in uniform with a caption reading KNOW YOUR ENEMY. At least these enemy soldiers were other human beings and clearly recognizable as such. If only there were some way of identifying our spiritual inner enemies so positively and definitely.

Once we learned of evil from what the church or other authorities told us, but then came the disillusionment of discovering they knew no more than anyone else, for they had just as many "baddies" among their ranks as any other groupings of humans. Now we have to face the fact that everyone has to discover his own Demons in himself and deal with these in a personal way. There is every reason however, that it would be best to combine and organize our efforts in the common cause of our "Freedom from Fiendishness". Why don't we try this before it is too late?

Chapter Nine

Exorcism by Effort

Most people at some time of their mortal lives (perhaps quite frequently) have considered the spiritual state of our mundane world and thought sadly about its unsatisfactory condition while regretting personal powerlessness to alter the situation. How many of us have said something like: "If only there were anything I could *do* about it!" Yet overwhelmed by the apparent magnitude of the task contrasted against their own ineffectiveness, millions of mortals passively permit the very forces they complain about so bitterly to flow through themselves un-checked and even augmented by energies exploited *en passant.*

Before we become too despondent about our life- affairs for altering them favourably, however, it may be as well to inquire whether we are really so useless as evil-wishers might like us to believe for their profit. Are we in fact helpless in the face of pitiless powers, or are we actually refusing to recognize our responsibilities as evolving entities, and do the life-duties assigned us by the creative consciousness behind our beings? Just what in this world can anyone do towards converting evilly directed energies into sounder spiritual courses? If it is clearly recognised that even the feeblest entity does indeed possess possibilities in this direction, then such a realisation should make the most miserable of lives some degree brighter and more bearable. Once a potential is actually appreciated the rest becomes a matter of willing and working.

First the problem of proportion has to be seen in a level light. Most people are frightened by the evident enormity of evil or other factors externally to themselves when contrasted with their own puny personal abilities. There is no need to be. Evil is not an external factor, anyway, although it seems so to an average observer accustomed to objectifying everything in terms of "otherness" to themselves. Evil operates along inner lines entirely as the cause of effects we consider bad relatively to ourselves. Although our personal pseudo-selves may seem so very small against this bad background, our true selves extend into infinite identity which is of more spiritual significance than all the evil we are likely to meet with as mortals. Therefore we should not measure the minute and inadequate abilities of our pseudo-selves against dwarfing proportions of evil directed against that end of our selves. Instead, we ought to awaken our awareness of inner identity which is capable of coping with any evil daring to threaten its existence. If evil is an inwardly directed energy, then it must surely be dealt with in those dimensions of living, and if our inner identities are spiritually superior to any evil, then we may rely upon that end of our selves to fulfill its natural function at its proper level. If we have linked our mortally manifested lives properly with this highest self-point, then it will naturally operate to some degree at this level also. So, when faced by all the evil this world might amass, let us know inside ourselves that we more than out match it in spiritual states of self it can never overcome while we intend otherwise.

It is perfectly true that a sufficient concentration of evilly intended energy directed against our pseudo-self ends of entity in this mundane world may break up our physical bodies, injure our associated mentalities, and inflict damage on our souls. Providing our spirits keep controlling contact with those sad effects they are quite repairable like the healing processes of a body infected by some illness. The "antigens" to ills caused by evil are derived from our deepest self-levels coming into close contact with divinity. If a condition of blockage or faulty contact exists between the "earthly" and "heavenly" ends of our entities, then a proper process of healing will not project through so far as our earth ends of entity are concerned, and they are likely to suffer accordingly. That is why it becomes so important when evil seems to threaten fearsomely, that we should counter-balance this by an instant inner call for contact with the only power operative through us which is able to neutralize what alarms us within our effective areas.

This is really what exorcism amounts to. Neutralizing evil in specific areas, whether those are human being or spatial locations. Endless nonsense has been written or supposed about the subject from time immemorial, but fundamentally it is the neutralization or displacement of some antipathetic energy by the intentional action of an agency capable of causing such an effect. It is obvious that extremely few, if any, ordinary humans have this ability in their conscious capacities as mere mortals. To become effective as exorcists, it is necessary to use the earth-end of entity purely as a focal point to project power derived from deep levels contacting divinity.

To attempt exorcism otherwise would be foolhardy or insane. It is utterly impossible for a human being already charged or infected with evil potency beyond the lowest degrees to act as an exorcising agency toward evil of much greater extent and energy. None with inhibitive evil in themselves can cast it out elsewhere. That is simple common sense.

No competent priest of any faith or initiate of any spiritual system would expect for one instant to exorcise even mild evils purely by their personal powers alone. What they have to do is expel or neutralize their own private evils and then clear their inner circles of consciousness until a sort of spiritual "laser-lens" is set up for use by that great power behind their beings symbolized as "living light". Without such a state of readiness it would be sheer madness to attempt exorcism of any kind. In any case, even if the "power of good" did concentrate through an unprepared and unsatisfactory agency it would automatically break down that agency like a bolt of lightning must needs burn out a hopelessly ineffective conductor foolishly offered for its passage. The art of exorcism lies entirely in creating those exact inner conditions which will facilitate the actions of forces needed to neutralize and/or change whatever evil may have come in focus. A priest might say, "1 cannot do this, but God acting through me can". An initiate would probably put it "The earth-end of my entity cannot do this of itself, but it may be made into a means for the will of my true identity to work through effectively". The principle in each case is the same. Careful arrangement of the lesser end of identity for specific use by the greater end to a far above average degree.

The significance of this can scarcely be overstressed. Ignorant enthusiasts who imagine they only have to wave wands or carry crucifixes about in order to expel evil forever deserve no less than the disasters they invite on themselves. About all which saves such from their foolishness is usually their utter insignificance and ineffectiveness. To put it bluntly, they are rarely worth the bother of dealing with since they constitute no threat whatever to the courses of genuine evil. Amateurs in the fringe-arts associated with magic who suppose they can abolish evil with a few paltry charms and antics only provide amusement or maybe mild annoyance to observant inner or outer entities. Perhaps they may be slapped down to size or insultingly ignored. They are unlikely to enjoy either event. Anyone trying to deal with evil outside their own self-circles while they yet hold dangerous traces of the principle in their hearts, merits whatever comes in consequence.

There is only one way in which evil may be abated, abrogated, or altogether abolished. By the power of perfection acting through suitable spiritual agencies capable of carrying enough of its energy for accomplishing this intention. The only reason why evil remains in this world among us is because the whole of mankind cannot provide adequate agencies for its elimination. All that allows evil to continue here is humanity. No God forces good on us, no Devil denies us divinity. We ourselves determine our own destinies by the decisions we make between those extremities of existence. If, as an aggregate, we encourage or permit the powers of evil to predominate throughout our world, it cannot possibly be bigger than all of us combined. What seems so huge to a single individual is really their own content of evil multiplied by all mankind. That is bad enough for anyone.

True exorcism of evil must start in the self-from top to bottom. That is the one and only way it is ever likely to leave this world for good. It is also the most practical and direct way for every soul to "do something" about the evil they complain of elsewhere - exorcise it in their own self-areas. By neutralizing it in themselves, they will not only lessen it to that degree for others, but will be able to act as agencies for the perfecting power of life in this world which needs every single such soul so very urgently. Therefore the real answer to those who bewail the evils of their times and lament their powerlessness to prevent this, is to ask "Have you exorcised yourself recently?" If we are not willing to clear evils from our own self-circles we have no right to complain of them elsewhere, nor any power to prevent them there either. The keys of exorcising our entire earth lie with each individual living therein.

A natural question here is "What is the use of my tackling evil in me while nobody else seems to bother? How far is my pathetic little effort liable to alter anything else?" The answer is that since all energies operate in "chain", and every living individual is one "link" of some specific "chain", effects of individual alterations with any self-state may be much more far-reaching than might be guessed by the "link" concerned. Let us take an analogy from electrical practice. We will suppose any circuit whatever, and assume the energy applied to it passes through a very fine wire at some important point. Now let us further suppose that each molecule of that wire has an ability of self-state determination like we have. We shall push this picture further by imagining what would happen if those relatively few molecules constituting the thinnest cross-section of the conducting wire decided to change their state into one which hindered or prevented the free flow of electrical force. That resolute minimum of molecules would thus interrupt the energy of an entire circuit, and alter or abrogate the whole arrangement of which they were very small parts indeed. This is purely an imaginative illustration of what could, not should, happen in our cosmic circumstances. It is possible for minimal individuals to make maximal differences within whatever life-framework forms their extensions of existence. Let us consider how one mutating microbe may proliferate into poison-producers which endanger or destroy an entire human organism. Again let us see the start of that organism physically initiated by a single sperm among millions fertilizing just one egg. Examples of this principle are everywhere we care to look for them.

There need be no doubt whatever in anyone's mind that if they could succeed in clearing their self-areas from the principle of evil to any considerable degree, they would make a most positive contribution towards decreasing its influence elsewhere. The usual difficulty lies with recognition of one's own content of evil, or obtaining an honest acknowledgment of its presence or presumed proportions within one's spiritual structure. It is only too easy to misread this entirely. Either it may be indignantly denied that any significant evil could possibly contaminate so pure a being, or feelings of luxuriant guilt may invent impossible amounts of sin in order to appear greater in pseudo-self size than is actually the case. It is very difficult indeed to estimate one's own evils, and the best thing to do is simply see these as principles of imperfection which call for alteration and act on that assumption.

An act of self-exorcism consists of "invoking", or calling up clearly into conscious focus whatever one would be rid of, then neutralizing this by a counter- measure of intention directing the course to be followed by the consciousness co-relating one's own inner cosmos. The important point of this process is that it must be truly, deeply, sincerely and wholeheartedly meant by whoever operates it. Otherwise there will be no result worth recording. This kind of exorcism only works to the degree of depth in anyone from which intention is directed. Moreover, it has to be initiated and carried into constancy by the individual himself in the true sense of the term. No well-meaning archangels or other entities of inner existence will come inside a self-circle and do the dirty work for which that self is entirely responsible. This is strictly a self-service affair altogether.

It might short-sightedly be objected: "But I have not the Dower to accomplish the task. It is too much for me. Where am I to get help?" Only the pseudo-self end of anyone would formulate such phraseology. Of course there is no such power prevailing in that pseudo-self, and it cannot possibly exorcise evils which exist there by its encouragement or passive permission. It is the "other end" of oneself from which energy to expel inherent evils may be derived, and there is but one way to obtain it - go up inside oneself and ask. Somewhere spiritually at the back of one's whole being is *whom* or *whatever* may be considered the creative cause of one's individual identity or selfhood. The focal point of consciousness normally turned objectively toward earthlife has to be reversed round and directed at this inner contact with divinity in order to receive responsive replies in return. Here we have to request our own selves at their points of origin to direct enough energy from the cosmic supplies with which they are, or should be, in close contact, so that a specific purpose according to an intention agreeable by both ends of our being may be accomplished. In older phraseology this might have read: "You have to find God inside you and ask or help in working whatever Will you share with each other

Therefore the primal point of self-exorcism is in deciding whether or not one really and truly intends to abate or expel the principle of evil from one's own autonomy. That is the crux of the entire issue. Perhaps facing up to this question and coming to a definite conclusion concerning it may not be a very pleasant inner adventure, yet that is what must be done if any further action should be contemplated. The key-query is just how much do we genuinely propose getting rid of evils by converting them otherwise in our self-areas, or how much are we merely making empty gestures and idle antics to camouflage inadequacy of intention or some other malfunction of character. Assuming such an inner probe has been made, a safe centre-stance might be taken that there truly is a sincere spiritual intention of decreasing evils existing in the self-circle by whatever degree the divine ends of our entities decide may be practical, considering present conditions prevailing. Once that proviso becomes acceptable, the way ahead clarifies a great deal.

That last point is important. The conversion rate of evil into good or any neutralizing process involved has a safety factor which varies a lot with different selves. Drastically sudden changes are likely to damage a self-structure very much. Rates of alteration ought only to take place within whatever limits of tolerance apply to the self specifically concerned. St. Augustine's famous prayer: "Please, God, make me pure and good - but not just yet, Lord! Not just yet", had a much deeper meaning than merely a pious witticism. Augustine meant what he said when he hoped to become better as a self at a safe rate of personal progress. We should do well to emulate his example. We need to exorcise our evils as fast as we dare, but at the same time we should realize there is a spiritual "speed-limit" for this which may not be exceeded without risk to the self-structure in question. Getting evils safely out of one self is often a more delicate and dangerous process than defusing a very intricate and deadly bomb mechanism. If proper procedures are not observed all the way effects can be most explosive in either comparable case.

Once more we are going to rely on the use of ritualized psychodrama for focussing the consciousness concerned with this process. Again it will be structured on the pattern of the Tree and related with the spiritual subject matter pertinent to our actions and meanings. That is one great advantage of the Tree-pattern. Any kind of ritual may be arranged with it, for it symbolizes life on all imaginable levels. It allows many variations of the same rite-theme, and can be readily adjusted for different viewpoints on identical ideas. Here, the whole plan of the Tree is geared to the single specific purpose of elimination of evil from the self-area, converting the energy exchanged into good, then directing this end-product into the "divine differential" or neutral point of poise which is our true "equation of entity". Once more the rite has been kept as simple as possible, but if elaborations are really felt needed, these may be added if and providing they support the rite-structure in its essential significance.

The essentials of the rite are these. Facing a material or mental image of the Tree and its Pillars, and armed with a physical or imaginary sword symbol, the operator salutes the Tree with the sword by a circle-cross sign, saying:

In the Name of the Wisdom   (touch forehead)

And of the Love   (touch heart)

And of the justice   (touch right shoulder)

And the Infinite Mercy   (touch left shoulder)

Of the one Eternal Spirit.   (clockwise complete circle covering those points and finish centre)

Amen   (Join hands prayer position)

Then with the sword in the "rest" position, point down, proclaim:

Throughout the whole of me

May evil banished be.

Negated into nil

According to my will.

Let good come in return

Until at last I learn

My perfect way of life

Above all inner strife.

All this rite should be taken on a slow, careful and very deliberate note, except perhaps the next section when the challenge to evil is exclaimed somewhat triumphantly:

O fatal pillars. Evil three.

I break your bondage and am free (sword gesture accordingly)

Coerced, compelled, condemned no longer.

Hard as you hold, my will is stronger.

The triple pillars I acclaim

As worthy to uphold my name

Are those of mercy-discipline

With moderation in between.

The sword is now brought up to the "carry" position, and the instruction boldly stated:

Now be my way made clear

In every vital sphere

As step by step I tread

My paths to light ahead.

Here the sword is used to point sphere by sphere from bottom to top of the Tree as each is called in turn. As evil is directed out, the sword is pulled back and pointed upwards as if it had literally picked the named evil out of the sphere and were flicking it off the point into NIL. As the good is invoked, the sword is pointed back to the sphere as if carefully conveying that particular quality there under guard. Then the sword is brought back to "carry" position in front of body centrally. Except where otherwise indicated, this action applies to all spheres commencing with the tenth.

10   **Materialism - fly.**

My kingdom is no lie.

9   **Unstable living - cease.**

Foundation firm - increase.

8   **Let greed in me decline**

That glory may be mine.

7   **May lust in me be dead.**

And victory live instead.

6   **Ugliness - depart.**

Rule, beauty, in my heart.

5   **Cruelty be done**

And discipline begun.

4   **Apathy - away.**

Compassion ever stay.

Here the abyss is addressed while the sword is held across it and the edgeways crossing imagined.

Be abyss of the lost

By knowledge safely crossed.

The sphere action continues:

3   **Antipathy must go**

     And understanding flow.

2   **Be stupidity rejected**

     As wisdom is elected.

1   **Atheism - never.**

     My spirit lives for ever.

All is now directed into the "infinite indefinite" above, and the sword waved slightly from side to side in an "opening" gesture.

0   **Be darkness put to flight**

     By perfect living light.

     So mote this be. Amen.

Sword back to "carry". The pronouncement is made-and meant:

There is no evil in me still

Which lingers but because I will.

Yet good in me increases

While latent evil ceases.

The sword is now rested, and a real inner attempt is made to rise toward the highest and finest point of Individual identity imaginable:

Now let me rise of right

Toward my highest light

Where my real self is found

In perfect peace profound.

Here is silence and stillness for as long as may be needed to establish and recognize consciousness with the contact sought. There is no point prolonging the period past its effective peak. Then the Tree is saluted with the sword briskly and the conclusion stated confidently and firmly:

So may it be with me.

Set forth upon my tree

That I shall live to be

My true identity.

Here (if known) the operator's "magical name" may be mentally formulated. Then the rite is closed with the circle-cross gesture:

In the name of the Wisdom [touch forehead]

And of the Love [touch heart]

And of the justice   [touch right shoulder]

And the Infinite Mercy   [touch left shoulder]

Of the one Eternal Spirit   [clockwise complete circle covering those points and finish centre]

Amen   [join hands prayer position]

Naturally this rite by itself will not instantly and entirely expel evil from anyone forever. What it does and will do is initiate the process of expulsion and re-balance from a conscious volitional level, decreasing effects of evil in our immediate self-area by the degree of intention involved. In other words, it begins to reduce evil within the self concerned, and thus makes a major contribution in favour of that individual cosmos. Small as this may seem, it may be increased by repetition of the rite either in full or by a condensed version. If persisted with despite disinclinations or difficulties, there will be a noticeable change in the characters of those working it periodically.

For those who like elaborating rites, much may be done with musical backgrounds, coloured lighting to suit the spheres, incense, costume and choreography. A combination of sword and rod may be used for banishing evil and invoking good. The other major symbols of shield, cup and cord can be introduced at the obvious points. Nor should it be forgotten that the Tree-plan aligns around the human body, and each item of it addressed objectively might also be lined mentally by the operator with the appropriate locations connected with themselves. There are very many ways this rite may be extended, if that would really help the individual work-

213

ing it. The rite could, of course, be worked by several people at once, each applying its structure to their own cases, because it cannot be used to exorcise anybody except oneself.

Once a practitioner of this psycho-drama is perfectly familiar with its pattern, it can be conveniently condensed into symbolic shorthand, as it were, for the benefit of expert users. This is one facet of ritualism deserving considerable study and practice. It means that rites which might take a great deal of time and trouble for average practitioners to perform can be structured down, as it were, so that experienced ritualists obtain the same effect with a basic minimum of equipment or effort. For example, reduced to its lowest common denominator or verbalism, this rite could read:

Evil out - in good.

May I balance as I should.

All necessary direction and internal activity is arranged by the volitional consciousness of the operator without external physical manifestation.

It is tempting to suppose that if this purely inner behaviour is effective, why bother about any externalized ritualism in dramatic form in the first place? Why not save a lot of time and money by keeping ritual principles entirely confined to inner levels of consciousness? What is the point of projecting them into physical practice? True enough, providing we were beings without bodies and did not extend our awareness into animal areas of consciousness. Ritual is for the purpose of linking these self-sectors of life into the spiritual scheme our rituals represent. However high-minded we like to believe we are, it is stupid to deny the incarnate ends of our entities while we are attached to this earth and evolution associated therewith. Whether we enjoy the duty or not we are responsible for the redemption of our humanity by directing it towards divinity. To do this successfully we need to speak spiritually in terms that our human animalistic natures appreciate. Rituals related with life-rhythms are about the most basic language of life they understand emphatically. Lecture a cat on lactation and she stares with contempt. Pour practical milk in a solid saucer and she comprehends completely. The first course is ridiculous, the second - ritual.

For those reasons, therefore, practically projected ritualism is an invaluable and irreplaceable part of magical procedures. Once the human ends of ourselves respond to the inner rhythms of the rites they participate in, they may be led carefully along those lines to the finer states of consciousness represented ritualistically. Conversely, they become accustomed to accepting spiritual suggestions and directions which reach them through the rites from sources otherwise too remote for such close contact. It is a simple fact of life that nothing brings the purely human constituents of people closer to their associated spiritual significance than principles of ritual. Not necessarily religious ritual at all. Any kind of ritual, social, political, ethnical or otherwise. Whatever behaviour pattern causes conscious recognition of other than material matters. In the case of magical ritualism, the aim is not only to link humans with their own higher possibilities but also to afford them opportunities of sharing themselves with other entities of different dimensional spiritual structures. Hence it has to connect with our ordinary levels of concrete creation in this mortal world. With competent and constant use, rituals may be condensed maybe to a gesture and a word or so, but they cannot be dispensed within principle while we have humanity on our hands, as it were.

Possibly the most powerful point in favour of this particular rite is that exorcism has to be brought as closely as possible to our earth-life levels because this is where evil concentrates mostly, and it is principally through these ends of entity that evil "gets into our systems". If we intend to exclude evil from our self- systems, therefore, we need to start turning it off as close to its source of supply as we can. There is no use being all "high pure spiritual" about it while nothing is done to prevent it ramping away through the embodied beings we are still attached to as spirits. Our incarnated ends of entity must know, feel and experience beyond all dispute that we resolutely intend self-exorcism throughout everything we are, and that includes "the beast whereon we ride", or our physical presentations of personality which act as our mundane agencies in this world. Since ritual as a principle is an age-old reliable method of influencing the earth-side of ourselves, then it is but common sense to employ it for this natural purpose.

It is well to remember also that there may be considerable "sales resistance" from the earthly ends of ourselves when exorcising influences are applied. They probably do not want to alter familiar forms of evil they have adapted with and become accustomed to. Nor are intenders and employers of evil, whether incarnate or otherwise, likely to be very enthusiastic about exorcism, which they view as a most anti-social practice having a poor effect on their profits. That much is only to be expected. Therefore, the most sensible course for intending self-exorcists to adopt is one of considerable discretion inwardly and outwardly. There is no gain what- ever to be made in arousing unnecessary and unhelpful antago- nism. If conflict becomes inevitable, then it must be dealt with responsibly and correctly, but it is best to avoid all the stupid squabbling and spiritual scuffling which in the long run can be much more damaging than one decisive issue faced and finished with.

Efforts at self-exorcism are therefore better kept for very private practice, and treated as being confidential be- tween one's own inner identity and that part of the self calling the operation into conscious expression on earth. The ideal aim should be that of exerting a steady and con- stant flow of spiritual energy on all self-areas affected by evil so that the action is tolerable and acceptable through- out the whole organism. Far more will be done that way than by making wild and spectacular attacks upon the principle of evil firmly ensconced in personal parts of the self where it has established something like squatters' rights. Even old-time exorcists realized that alternative accommodation should be offered to ejectable demons, though they seldom had anything more attractive to sug- gest than hell-fire, or the Red Sea, or even less likely places to entice homeless hellions. A more modern exorcist might be perceptive enough to offer the opportunity of a holiday from hell in that deep peace which passes all un- derstanding. Our concepts of punishment have changed for the better. Rather than retribution, which cannot possi- bly alter evil already in the past, it is surely more sensible to institute character changes which will avoid future rep- etitions. That is the principle on which modern exorcism works, whether with humans or non-incarnating entities. Containing evil by an energy field which carefully consumes it and absorbs its potentials into other expressions of power. In self-terms, this means "eating up" our own evil, digesting it, and eventually excreting it as harmless humus to fertilize our Tree of Life and promote its growth towards perfection.

Once the determination to promote this process has been carried into our working consciousness as humans by means of magical or other kinds of ritual, it will begin the banishment of evil, providing it is pushed quietly and steadily along with constant and cautious pressure. Repetitions of the rite in full or its briefest abbreviated form should be made at enough regular intervals to give a sense of continuity and purposeful progression. It may easily be worked in the mind and body together as a walking-rhythm or Inner accompaniment to any suitable repetitive activity. This old employment of "magical muttering" or "mantras" is sadly neglected these days, and might well be redesigned to suit modern requirements. Formerly it was more widely practiced, and when people were engaged in mechanical tasks they frequently set their next level of consciousness into comparable *inner cycles* having specific spiritual meanings. Above this again, of course, another height of awareness was reached which was normally beyond close contact by those who had to engage their attention with earthly activities. Rosaries operate on this principle, but it may be applied to almost any physical pursuit of a regular kind. We might do our self-exorcism while walking along, for instance, or using a sewing machine. In parentheses, it seems rather a pity that sewing machines are unsuitable for the lovely old rite of making a "blessed shirt". This had to be made by hand for a loved wearer, and each single stitch must be accompanied by a prayer or in- vocation that the recipient might be blessed perhaps in some particular way. Not one stitch was to be missed or the charm failed. Comparable exercises might be arranged for eliminating evil from self-systems.

It may be interesting to note also in passing here that the intentional relationship of physical symbols and behaviour with metaphysical equivalents or associations is the fundamental key to successful ritualism. The idea is to commence carefully with a few attempts in this direction, and then so extend and improve that in the end one's whole life becomes a constantly expanding consciousness of inner realities linked with outer items. That is ritualism in a nutshell. Recognizing the spiritual linkage of all material appearances. Not only this but also the ability to arrange and employ such a faculty for particular purposes. In a way it is an inversion of the cosmic process by which we "fell" into materialization ourselves. Originally conscious in purely spiritual terms, the *spirit of man* became more and more interested in lower and lower levels of life until eventually it was caught up by these to an extent of losing direct touch with inner identity and accepting partial projections into animal incarnations as established methods of becoming an entity. Now, mankind should be "on the way back". Our material manner of living ought to offer us a means of changing our consciousness over to the inner courses which will lead us toward that spiritual state which is really our most natural type of life. To realize what we-should become, we had best begin by remembering what we were, and since ritualism helps us to find reminders of this everywhere on earth, we should surely value it as it duly deserves.

This most emphatically does not mean we ought to reject or despise all material affairs outright for any reason whatever. Our overall withdrawal from the scenes of incarnation is best accomplished as a constant of evolutionary growth and development, not as a violent severance which only inflicts spiritual damage likely to result in re-involvement with matter in much worse ways. It is largely a question of viewpoint as to whether we regard spirit as a means of materializing ourselves, or matter as a means of spiritualization. Between these two extremes lies the razor-edge of identification with whatever ultimate reality we truly intend to become.

Not all the evil in existence can prevent this, nor all the good we might ever do guarantee it. Everything depends upon our learning to live in line with the identity of our true selves on all levels of life. Since this is the metaphysical equivalent of aiming directly at divinity in the straightest possible way, the symbol for the process is that of light. Outwardly, light is the constant of our cosmos, and inwardly it serves the same parallel purpose, which is why so many spiritual systems use it as a short of "homing-beacon" toward their truth targets. Therefore, let that be our last consideration in this series of study.

Chapter Ten

The Perfection Principle

Look at our lives on this earth what way we will, it amounts to the most muddled mixture of "do-badders" and "do-gooders" keeping each other going by exchanges of energy everywhere. Often enough in individuals who combine both principles in them- selves while never reconciling these for any better purpose of living. So many people see life as a sort of bat- tleground between the principle of good and evil with an ultimate triumph for good in the dim and distant future when "all will be well with the world". This is nothing more than futile fantasy, sad though it may be to recog- nize the fact. Intelligent evildoers make their biggest profits out of foolishly generous do-gooders. Likewise intelligent good-willers convert the ill effects of evil into some of our greatest blessings, which in their turn are lia- ble to reversion, and so the "game of life" goes on with the score standing at anyone's guess. If we cannot, or will not, learn to live by some better spiritual system than that we shall never reach any higher state of being than our present one, and that would be quite literally "a fate worse than death".

This means we need to discover (or rather recover in ourselves) a very different spiritual standard of life from that by which we have been misruling ourselves for so long. There is no question of something new being set up, but of our very oldest and most original life-principle being restored to its upright position as it were. Symbolically this would be our "resurrection" or "raising" from the metaphorical mire wherein mankind has wallowed so wilfully since our first fall". We need to get off the ground, wipe the muck out of our inner eyes and find out how to look around us by the light which was shining about our darkness all the time. Sooner or later, those intending to identify their true selves with Something infinitely greater than the whole of mortal mankind will ever be, must learn how to stand even shakily on their equivalents of feet and start looking at life as an experience leading to nowhere except their own inclusive identification with the spirit of life itself.

The Edenic (relating to Garden of Eden) myth indicates that our spiritual state of perfection lies beyond the bounds of both good and evil. Our troubles were reputed to have begun by an act of evil which called for an act of good as compensation. This good, following evil, immediately created conditions in which more evil flourished and such unceasing cycles have accompanied us all along our trail of time. In this sense it is good that keeps evil going, and well do expert evildoers know and exploit that fundamental. Where else would they gain their needed supplies? Conversely, a convinced do-gooder welcomes the challenge of evils affording scope for his preferred type of self-expression. Perhaps unconsciously they are each other's allies to that extent, and while they struggle for supremacy in this or any other world, humanity as a whole remains imperfect and unhappy. Collectively, we can only become the aggregate of our individual attitudes and awareness to life which determine whatever activities we engage with as expressions of our existence. Everything begins and ends in individuality, so if anything is to be done concerning the condition of our entire earth-living this has to come through individual intentions and directions of inner energy. There is no other way.

Probably the hardest part of this process is realizing its possibility. Looking at our small pseudo-self ends of entity we tend to compare these with the enormity of everything else and become so discouraged by what we see from this angle that we just go on drifting with the general tide of mass-mankind. Maybe worse, we enthusiastically commence one-man wars with the majority of mankind which are automatically lost before they begin. Eventually we might learn better spiritual sense between these two wrong courses, but it is best to avoid both and go steadily along with the one main life- motivation which should be our constant concern, making ourselves into what and whom we are meant to be according to the inner intention behind our beings. That is the essential of everyone's life, and all else is incidental. First things first, and the remainder will fit in place around them.

Every single soul coming to realize this fundamental factor of life consciously and acting in accordance with its implications is of the highest possible importance in the spiritual scheme for ultimate perfection of our species. Each individuant (or initiate as they used to be called) acts as an automatic agent for what could be termed the perfecting power. It is not so much what they *do* which counts, but what they actually *are*. That is of paramount spiritual significance, and the whole story of initiation, or the "way of light" as a life-constant. Living by neither good nor evil, but by a balance of being which transcends both principles as a truth extending beyond the limits of either. In a completely correct cosmos, evil would be inadmissible and good entirely unnecessary. Perfection needs neither in its paradise.

It should scarcely be necessary to note that such a state of exemption from good and evil alike is hardly attainable for any ordinary member of mankind. Nevertheless, once this principle of perfection is appreciated, however distantly, it becomes theoretically possible to set up symbolic simulations which will positively help humans intending advancement along these lines to achieve some degree of semblance with the inner actuality aimed at. That is how ritual practice works. Some intended state or condition is presented as a suitable symbolic pattern in which people may participate with inner intelligences associated therewith. This results in specific energy - exchanges tending to project the purpose of the pattern into other dimensions of living. A concrete example of this might be an architect's drawing-board process regarded as the requisite ritual for producing subsequently solid edifices. So with spiritual equivalents. If we are able to work out a symbolic synthesis of the spiritual structure we intend producing in ourselves or otherwise we shall at least accomplish the vital preliminaries most likely to lead us along the path of our choice. Here we need to set up something which will both simulate and stimulate our self-sense of ultimately reaching a point of perfection past all good or evil in *peace profound.*

To become free from the evils so evident in this earth might seem a glorious proposition to all who suffer from them. Everyone has their own ideas about the wonderful sorts of life we could live without evil, and the beautiful heavens we would build as compensations for whatever hells we have endured. How few humans realize that these very heavens holding every good we ever craved for would inevitably produce much worse hells of a different kind leading us back - to the beginning of another "fall" again? We cannot escape hell without avoiding heaven also. Heavens and hells are but postponements of each other. Those who look no higher or lower than these self-states will metaphorically chase their own tails from one to the other until widening light or maybe sheer boredom opens fresh inner frontiers for them.

The fundamental working of the spiritual process we are seeking, therefore, is one of "overcoming evil with good" and then neutralizing the resultant energy in order to produce Perfection. Merely overcoming evil with good is not enough, because more evil will subsequently arise. Unless good is successfully negated into the perfectibility principle after absorption of evil, the whole expenditure of energy will be largely wasted. That is why it becomes increasingly important for humans to recognize this central concept as the spiritual standard with which mankind may measure its own stature in the future.

It may be very difficult for a humanity which has been conditioned for so many generations into "good-evil" classification of consciousness to grasp the significance of this concept at all. We have been so accustomed to thinking "I ought not to do that because it is wrong, and I should do this because it is right" (or vice versa if we are real "baddies"), that we usually fail to find our way correctly between both courses. Few indeed even suspect the existence of this "centreline" which should lead right through life into ultimate light. Finding and keeping such a self-course is what initiation ought to be about. Learning how to live independently of good or evil as emancipated entities bound by neither because of becoming "tied to truth".

Hard as it might be to appreciate what this means, it has yet to become the basis of our whole spiritual excursion into the areas awaiting our forthcoming awakening as heirs to a "kingdom" of infinite possibilities. Already there are noticeable stirrings which indicate some degree of awareness in more than a few mortals. Let devout souls pray, and others hope that any actual "awakening" comes quietly and naturally as a normal act of evolution. In times to be, perhaps not so far away as generations go, this world may yet be the habitation of humans among whom evil is almost non- existent because of being both unfashionable and unprofitable, besides having been outgrown as unsatisfactory means of self-expression. Similarly will good be surpassed by the sheer perfection of people and things becoming as they should according to the "initiating intention" within them. Impossible? Not as all. Unlikely? That remains for us to decide for ourselves.

It is quite certain that dedicated evildoers would not welcome such a prospect at all, since they see no profit in it and would undoubtedly do everything possible in opposition. While evil pays high dividends it will fight with all it has to preserve its possessions and powers. No less should be expected. For similar fundamental reasons dedicated do-gooders would equally fight to preserve the pure and high-minded principles they believe in. As they see things, good is the way they want this world to be. Everyone happy to order, no suffering, no inequalities, endless entertainments, everything wonderful, and glory be to God in the highest! A sort of divine dictatorship, whether God is seen as a spiritual being or a human political autocracy. Either possibility seems a poor spiritual outlook for our future acceptance, and the only conceivable "escape route" lies along the light-line we have been considering. If enough individuals proceed carefully and calmly to clear this inner way for themselves, plenty of parallel paths will open up for others to follow on their accounts later. All it needs is for those who see and recognize the vital importance of this central concept to begin consciously lining up their lives with it, and that would successfully "bring through" enough of it into earth-level areas where others could then "pick it up" for themselves subsequently - if they so willed.

Let no mistaken ideas arise about this being some kind of salvation scheme which could be imposed upon mankind "for our own good" or any such notion whatever. Humanity will not be "saved" from or by whatever derives from compulsions, coercions, incentives, inducements or anything other than individual inner choice coming from contact with the divine identity behind each being. It is true that every avatar, sacred king, and all others who "gain Godhood" even in minor degrees, substantially improve and increase the chances of everyone else on earth to follow the same divine direction, but in the end we have to save or damn our- selves. That is our universal ultimatum, however the spiritual shock of facing it may affect us. At the same time it should also be realized that inner resources for accomplishing our ultimate attainment are not only available for the asking on such specific grounds but are virtually infinite.

Deep down, away from our merely mortal pseudo-self levels of life, we connect up with inner self-sections of identity which link with other living beings that classify as "immortals" by our standards of experience. Ultimately we connect with divinity itself, *WHAT OR WHOEVER THAT IS*. It is from those inner resources that we may derive and utilize the energies we need to apply the process of perfection through ourselves. From the same source we may make contacts of consciousness which will enable us to assist this application intelligently and correctly. Learning to live "centre- conceptually" will put us in constantly closer touch with those inner life-links which matter most to anyone intending transcendence of their own mortality. That is its spiritual significance to initiated souls, and why its practice becomes so important.

The principles of the practice are that instead of reacting to externals of life from our lower self-levels alone, the inner paths by which these affect us from outside are intentionally pushed right back as close as possible to the "nil-nucleus" of eternal entity around which our beings are built, so that *IT* will direct appropriate reactions or else equate the energy other- wise. Conversely, instead of externalising inner energies purely for relatively petty purposes projected from our lowest levels, the directing centre releasing these into circulation, so to speak, is raised progressively higher toward our spiritual self-points concerned solely with the process of perfection.

On the Tree of Life, this is known as the "middle pillar" practice. That is to say, lining up our material manifestations with the spiritual spheres of stability *(Yesod)*, harmony *(Tipherethl,* knowledge *(Daath),* and divine identity *(Kether),* so that all these permit the passage of Perfect Light from the infinite *(Ain-Soph-Aur)* above all.

In a sense, like lining up a series of lenses, so that when their exact centres co-related correctly a laser-beam came into operation effectively. In fact, we need to achieve the spiritual equivalent of that precise physical phenomenon. Nothing less is likely to cut through the deliberate "darkness" disseminated by the Tree of Evil counterparts of atheism, ignorance, ugliness and instability projected into sheer materialism.

There are very many "middle pillar" exercises and magical methods of that nature described in modern works dealing with practical Qabalism. Repetition of these here will not be very helpful. So what we shall consider is a sort of epitomatic exercise in ritualised form designed for "centring in" consciousness from good-evil divergence to a straight spiritual "perfection path". It is not exactly an easy effort to begin with, but with repetition it becomes increasingly effective. Only the "bare bones" will be outlined as essential. Elabotations and extensions are always possible from personal preferences so long as basic principles are faithfully followed.

First of all, it is necessary to make a concept concerning the nil-principle by which we shall equate our energies into a neutral central-control condition. Though we can- not think of *nothing*, we can still symbolize it. Since cosmos has three main constituents we recognize as time, space and events, we must metaphorically reduce these to *nothing*. Here is one useful method. Take the sense of time, and broaden it out indefinitely. Try and see what one mortal lifetime amounts to from a view- point of uncounted millennia. Start gradually thinking what an hour of life seems like from experience of a week, then a month, then a year, and so on. Keep pushing this until some realization is felt of how the intensity of any given moment fades into nothing relatively to infinite time even though it will keep its individuality forever. All becomes nullified in total time, and it is an awareness of that factor which should be aimed for just here. When some degree of this becomes possible, turn to space, and figure how all our bodily beings are constructed from molecules, atoms, electrons, and ultimately pure energy. Imagine a condensation of such space into infinite nothing inside the self until irreducible identity is reached. Try and feel a semblance of reduction to an absolute reality beyond which only unbeing could be possible. What would all the space our bodies occupy and move around in seem like from that angle of observance? If any conception of this can be reached, turn next to events and try and see everything not as a series of happenings strung together serially, but simply as a *whole* having one value for the entire lot. If everything that happened to oneself in this world for a complete incarnation were aggregated together as a "lump of life", what would it be worth? Supposing all that had ever happened with everyone in this world since we came here were put into one piece of sameness? What would relatively be the value of one individual' s experience of events at any selected second? All these and similar thinkings should be persevered with until a concept of relative nullity contrasts oneself with the rest of creation.

It must be realised this is actually an infinite enhancement of self-significance comparable with a proportional decrease in pseudo-self importance. By "not being" as we will, we may "be" as we will otherwise, if indeed that is our true intention. The zero of "not- being" or nil must come first, however, and that is why we have to learn "zeroing-out" as the preliminary prac- tice to "initiating-in". Once it becomes possible to hold some kind of symbolic nil-concept as a "background state" of consciousness for a while, the remainder of our ritualized exercises may be proceeded with.

The next thing we shall need is a simple materialized symbol of the nil-state. A hand gesture makes a useful medium because hands are not only expressive, but are also generally available. As the accepted sign of nil is the circle of zero, let our gesture be that of raised arms above the head with fingertips touching in mid-air. This elementary position should convey an idea of consciousness (the head) surrounded by an eternal equity of nil (the arm-circle). To indicate "release into nil", the arms may be brought steadily down to the sides of the body in order to make a wide circle-sweep inclusive of the whole person. If the breath is also exhaled slowly during this move it will help its significance.

Another gesture will be needed to show the holding of whatever particular point or problem it is intended to neutralize. The natural movement here is of reaching out slightly with both hands forward and sideways a little as if the right hand were grasping all the good of the issue while the left hand took hold of its evil. Then both hands are brought together centrally in a cupped position as if perhaps a bird or butterfly were most carefully held captive prior to release. This move takes a good deal of practice by itself, as will soon be discovered during first attempts. The thing to do is call any particular point to mind as clearly as possible, then try and take hold of it mentally as a matter of both good and ill as a *whole* while symbolizing this with the hand gestures. No attempts should be made to analyse or opinionate whatever it may be. Just grasp it and hold it as it appears.

The next key-gesture is that of the "perfecting poise" or central control to be held so that this principle "divinely dominates" the self-situation. This is undoubtedly the bringing together of both hands centrally, palms pressed together and fingertips up-wards in the well-known "praying hands" position. The fingers and thumbs of both hands should meet *exactly,* and it is most important that firm pressure should be applied so that the hands have to be kept together as an act of intention rather than by their own inertia. The arms, of course, are held close to the body and the fingertips about below chin level. While holding this position, a sense of "balanced being" should be invoked, as if the one single issue of spiritual importance in life were becoming as perfect as possible independently of all else except that precise purpose of the true self behind one's own being. This gesture, too, should be practised again and again until it "comes clear" in the consciousness and helps to hold its signified self-state when employed for that reason.

With these three main gestures practised and made workable they can be combined and built up into a somewhat more elaborately structured rite. In passing, it is interesting to note how many of these wonderfully significant and practical activities have "died on their feet" among orthodox religious ritualists. Performed as empty observances they are no more than maybe quaint antiquities, and yet they still have the potential for being re-powered by anyone capable of interpreting them on inner levels. Perhaps one day there will be an awakened investigatory interest in such survivals, and fascinated explorers will find a whole "lost world" awaiting rediscovery from clues which were with us all the time.

To "react in" from any external consideration to the

self, use the "grasping" gesture while taking hold of the imagined objective, lift it up above the head and "release" it into the nil symbolized by the circling arms. Neutralize as much as possible in this personal area, then drop the arms slowly to the sides while exhaling breath. The idea to be held during this is of allowing everything to become equated out into the infinite nil of all life. Then begin to "pick up poise" by bringing the fingertips together centrally until they come together in their positive position of power between heart *(love)* and head *(wisdom)*. Concentrate on achieving whatever may be the best life-attitude from the true inner identity toward the subject of the rite. After an affirmation to this effect, sweep the hands out sideways in a "welcoming" gesture, and revert to ordinary consciousness again.

For "reacting out" an inner intention start with hands at bottom position and invoke self-awareness of infinite nil relationship. Carry hands up above head and circle with fingertips. Invoke intention of own true identity on given issue or simply as a pure spiritual principle. Still keeping fingertips together, bring hands down centrally before face and fold palms together in powerwise position. *Inhale* during this. Make affirmation. Lastly, push hands forward and outward separately while exhaling as if opening a door leading into active living. Return to normal average awareness and pursuits.

The verbalized conscious elements of this rite should be kept as succinct and "packed" as possible. For example:

Commence:

In the Name of the Wisdom (Head)

And of the Love (Heart)

And of the justice (R. Hand)

And the Infinite Mercy (L. Hand)

Of the one Eternal Spirit (Circle centre)

Amen.

Grasp issue:

Let good or ill be what it will

Yet strife must cease

In perfect peace.

Negating:

Therefore, abate - equate - negate.

To power as a potential state.

Invoke Identity:

O true one that am I

Thou art my life for aye.

I in thou and thou in me

Make what I am meant to be.

Counter-poise:

May all I am most willingly

Prove my perfectibility.

Relate with Life:

What it will be as I

Let life itself reply.

All being brought to naught

But as it truly ought.

In the Name of the Wisdom   [touch forehead]

And of the Love   [touch heart]

And of the justice   [right shoulder]

And the Infinite Mercy   [left shoulder]

Of the one Eternal Spirit   [clockwise complete

circle covering those points and finish centre]

Amen   [Join hands prayer position]

This again can be condensed to a "shortened version" in perhaps this form. Bring hands together as clenched fists touching body and each other about lower chest level while imagining the polarized principle of any issue being grasped. Verbalize:

Good and Ill.

Form the two hands into a Zero-circle by opening out so that fingers and thumbs are pressed together as if grasping a circular object from opposite sides. Look at this "emptiness held" and with appropriate mentalisation, verbalize:

Be still as nil.

Convert the finger-thumb circle to a triangle by straightening out the fingers and thumbs. See this as the point of poise between two divergent lines, and verbalize the idealisation as:

True will be done.

Bring the palms and fingers together in the "praying" power-poise position while identifying with the inherent "Divine Intention" and verbalize:

As perfect one.

Amen.

As a finishing gesture, palms and fingers may be rubbed together lightly and briskly.

By this time is should be realized that an important principle of practical ritualism is conversion of conscious content to progressively condensed symbolism while "pressurising" the effective energy accordingly. In spiritual terms this is not unlike making a build-up to sub- critical mass in order to obtain a potential of nuclear power. Another analogy would be that of winding a spring mechanism to drive a clock for a prolonged period. One is reminded of the familiar, "Peace! The charm's wound up", in *Macbeth,* and wonder if old-time witches knew their business better than modem claimants to the title. That is very much what these rites accomplish. "Winding up", or compressing consciousness to a point where correct triggering and application will release energy along specific paths of purpose.

At this juncture any "un-magically" minded person might be forgiven for saying: "I never heard a larger load of rubbish in my life. You twiddle your fingers, say a bit of nonsense, do some wishful thinking, hope for the best and call that magic? I could think of less printable terms with half the effort", or words to that effect. Would they be correct? No. Merely incapable of extending consciousness beyond the most superficial levels of inner experience. What have they missed in this instance, and will always miss until awareness becomes awakened along other physical lines? Let us see for ourselves.

By means of these, or similarly structured rites, patterns of conscious energy are constructed and employed with intention by individuals and intelligences sharing common schemes of cosmic creation. This applied energy has definite effects. Those may be, and usually are, imperceptible to our normal sensors, or beyond calculation by any instrumentation available to us at present. Because we cannot yet calculate or determine the effects of conditioned consciousness operating on our deepest life-levels this does not mean they are either insignificant or unimportant. In fact, all far-seeing indications are that this makes life-and-death differences to our whole existence. As we evolve, this becomes increasingly evident to anyone with inner eyes raised even a degree above ground level. In time to come for us, it will prove a major factor in our living methods, but for *now* it is still magic.

Consider for a moment or so the virtual sea of conscious energy we live in just as ordinary humans on earth. All the millions and millions of people thinking, emoting, feeling, and otherwise altering the common state of consciousness we all share in this time-space-event continuum. Consciousness is *energy* and as such *effective*. It affects all we do, and all we are. There need be no doubt of that. The majority of humans are mainly passive permissives of consciousness, allowing it to process around them most of their lives while they adapt accordingly with its persuasive pressures and universal urges. How many are prepared to use consciousness creatively enough on deeply deliberate levels of life to make much real difference for themselves and con- sequently others connected with them? Most people very rarely, some seldom, and few indeed frequently or forcefully enough to cause any spectacular spiritual changes among us. So who makes the patterns in the programs of consciousness which move along any predictable lines?

Over our wide areas of activities, these patterns principally arrange themselves from our average aggregate of awareness, but they may be directionally influenced by deliberate insertion of intentions at strategic spiritual points. By and large, this is generally done by 'ultra-bad' or 'ultra-good' affectors of human actions. Only the sheer mass-inertia of mankind saves us from swinging too wildly in either direction, but already there are signs of possibly dangerous changes taking place in this somewhat uncertain safety factor. There are not enough intentional "balancers" as yet operating among us to guarantee any satisfactory state of spiritual security for our future as incarnating entities of this earth. Whatever may be true outside our immediate areas of existence, the fact remains that we have to concern ourselves with human affairs as they presently are in order to form a future worth having in any condition of consciousness.

As things are, we need more and more skilled spiritual "'balancers" with an ability of evening- out the energies of existence being flung forcibly around the inner fields of living between good and bad extremities. That is the most necessary magic for the whole of mankind in our world today, tomorrow and its foreseeable future. Balancers. Equators of inner energy. Once called "mediators". Sometimes even "saviours".

That is precisely what the rites we have been working out should be concerned with. The equation we need to solve the spiritual "riddle of the Sphinx" or enigma of existence which man has been bothered by since the beginning of our entry to this earth. Each one of us is a vital integer of that *master problem,* and-its ultimate solution lies in the integers' arrangement of themselves so as to spell out the "lost word" which will be the complete cosmic answer. Therefore let each integer look to its own alignment with that total truth by the light in which it perceives *perfect peace.* If some simple form of magically motivated ritual procedure will serve for focussing the needed forces of consciousness towards such a purpose, then this provides more than justification for those prepared to practice or observe such a rule. It becomes even an obligation for whoso recognizes its importance.

Every single balancer in this world becomes an incarnate mediator of the perfecting power behind the mystery of mankind. Perhaps "spiritual stabilizers" might be a better description. Under any name they are likely to make the vital difference between divinity or doom for humanity as a whole engaged with evolution at earth-levels of life. The more our population increases fatally towards critical mass, the more need for a wider distribution of specialist stabilizers to maintain sub- critical pressures and eventually bring these to balance in line-line living. That is how important the fundamentals of what we have been ritualizing are to this world. Whether we put them into practice by these particular rites, or invent others of any species whatever, scarcely matters so long as the inner effects they are intended to achieve are actually carried into cosmic circulation. As the given rites stand, they will at least provide a launching platform for anyone inclined to explore inner dimensions of life on more than material levels.

It is almost time we woke up to ourselves as evolving entities of life struggling spiritually in our sleep while we dream of what might or might not be accomplished by our mundane manifestations incarnate in flesh forms. "Incarnate" literally means "in meat-form", and until we realize the inner and individual nature of our true identities, we need expect no higher type of living. Surely there must be many souls alive growing very tired of being bashed between "goodies" and "baddies" for no particular sound spiritual reason, who are anxious to set up self-states of their own and make responsible relationships with all other entities included in the ultimate entity of everyone? Selves capable of structuring their power-patterns for acting as the stabilizing agents we need so very urgently in this era of human spiritual history. Selves of sufficient stature for breaking any bonds shareholders of the evil tree are likely to set as snares for captivating consciousness. Selves who seek liberation through the Tree of Life and are willing to walk the way of poise that points to *perfect peace profound.* Somewhere among us incarnately or otherwise there have to be these "companions of cosmos", holding humanity more or less together in some semblance of shared spiritual shape. Can they continue to cope with currently increasing pressures and exigencies which mount almost from one moment to the next with alarming increments? Anyone is entitled to guess, but none worthy of true self-status can afford the slightest degree of complacency or any irresponsible assumptions. Affairs are too serious for any such spiritual slackness.

We have studied the Tree of Evil in broad outline sufficiently to see a need for further investigation in detail at some later instance. We have learned that the energies it employs or hi-jacks from permissive humans may be converted into good usages. Best of all we should by now have realized that a still superior level of spiritual life is not only possible, but must positively become practical if we are truly to survive as the Selves we should become by the end of time and preferably sooner than that. This is not really a "new outlook" at all, but the regaining of our oldest original life-look. It amounts to recovering our "lost" innocence in which state injury of any kind simply becomes an utter impossibility. That may be a difficult or even as yet an unacceptable concept for many mortals to deal with, but nevertheless if it comes not among us on earth, none can hold harm from us forever.

So how is anyone to claim inclusion in the select self-circles of cosmic companionship? Only by one way. Entry earned through adequate and accurate self-structurisation. There is no alternative because this is the middle method between all possible alternatives. It means coming to the end of every side-issue leading to good or ill on the binary branches of our Life-Tree, and reaching a point above all else where nothing except perfection is possible. Remote as this may seem to us on earth, our pathway leading thence begins with such simple things. A train of thought. Inward excursions. Observant outlooks. A sense of purpose prolonged past incarnatory possibilities. Inner experiences linked with external symbolism, preferably available easily. Maybe sunlight on a cloud, a candle shining softly by itself, a whispered Name, a significant scent, a melody or sonic sequence. Anything at all leading life lightward for inwardly awakening individuants. Something perhaps as easy as a remembered ritual for conditioning consciousness according to inmost intentions. It is always the little things in Life that matter most, because they constitute the basis of which the very biggest become built. The beginning of all "greats" is in the "leasts", and that is where we have to look for the makings of maximum light - in its barely perceptible divine spark within each of us. So does cosmic companionship start.

It is interesting to think that the most devastating atomic explosion or most potent power-pile we have, commences with the specialized behaviour of a single atom which communicates forthwith through others in a chain-reaction until the entire Energy released accomplishes its maximum effort. So it can also be with we humans, for far more peaceful purposes. All it takes is the right initiating action among those able to commence communication chains of inner consciousness along correct lines of actual spiritual living. So far we have seen how our world reacts with both good and bad instigators of such energy-effects. Now our greatest need is for neutralisers in sufficient supply and properly distributed throughout the whole of humanity to act adequately as spiritual safety-factors for us all. For these to be forth- coming, they will have to recognize this need and their own ability of its fulfilment in themselves, then continue as inwardly and individually directed.

Above all, it is necessary to realize that there *IS* behind our beings a divine intention of perfection inherent in everyone *IF* we are willing to live with and by it. This does not demand, compel, coerce, or otherwise insist on our acceptance of it. So far as we are concerned it is neutral relatively to all our extremities, and aligning ourselves with it is our supreme act of spiritual equation. Alternatively, we condemn ourselves to conflicts and survival struggles for as long as we are stupid enough to stay in such states or until we abandon existence altogether by what amounts to spiritual suicide. Such are the "facts of life" from a cosmic viewpoint. Those who already are, or who are yet becoming cosmic companions, know what to do with that basic information. Others have to learn what they can as they will, though the way is always open for anyone to find for themselves in themselves, however they may be helped.

Granted an adequate "network of neutralisers" functioning throughout this world, we could face our human future with far more confidence than our present position justifies. There are certainly signs to some extent that more than a few members of our youngest generation seem to have been born with an inherent instinct of this ability in themselves. They could yet live long enough by the Tree of Life to control the cultivators of the Tree of Evil sufficiently for helping humanity as a whole past this peak-period of peril. No spiritual situation is hopeless while there are capable souls devoting their lives to dealing with it. These souls have a very special task indeed. Literally they will act as "stand- ins" for that particular spiritual power concerned with what was once called the "salvation" of mankind, or saving the best in us from destruction by the worst in us so that what is true in us will at last come to light.

A long time ago "saviours", or sacred kings, came singly into incarnation for the sake of their particular people. Now the power behind those personifications has to be scattered much more widely among a selection of suitable individuals, a little to each, as it were, so that the overall effect is both constant and consistent throughout our whole human area. In a way this could be described as a "second coming", insofar as all previous focal points of the same power might be considered a "first". This time, however, we should not expect the same psycho-drama to be presented in precisely similar scripting. There will be many incarnations, massacres of many innocents, trainings in many trades, dissemination of widespread teachings, faithful friendships and brutal betrayals. Many will be condemned and metaphorically crucified because of beliefs. Though they must die physically yet shall their spirits immediately resurrect in those reborn to replace them. The same old story forever told in new terms. It is the legend of life itself, unfolding another version of its most magical myth for every generation of mankind to experience. No deliberately manufactured "gaps" can possibly exist between individuals of all generations who speak the same spiritual language of light because they belong to the same inner family of faith. These are the connected "children of cosmos" who must lead forward to whatever future may be worth working for in this and finer worlds. Blessed be they who are asking *nothing* for all. Let whoever understands this keep counsel faithfully.

The end of every book should be but the beginning of its true telling in the realization of every reader. So be it now. If only one degree of difference has taken place in those who have followed so far from the first word until this point, then that much of its mission is already accomplished. There is only one last word really worth saying to anyone, so let this be said with the utmost sincerity and maximum of meaning possible between fellow members of mankind. It is:

PEACE.

Index

Kima Global Publishers is an independent publishing company based in Cape Town.

We specialise in *Books that Make a Difference to People's Lives*.

We have a unique variety of Body, Mind and Spirit titles that are distributed throughout South Africa, the U.K., Europe, Australia and the U.S.A.

Among our titles you will find Non-Fiction, Healing, Esoterics, Philosophy, Parenting, Business coaching, Personal Development, Creative workbooks and Visionary Fiction.

Kima Global Publishers helps to shape and groom new writers to become successful authors.

Robin Beck

We at Kima Global Publishers trust that you enjoyed this book. You will find others by visiting our website http://www.kimaglobal.co.za from where you may place an order. Particularly we have pleasure in recommending the following which contains chapters on Kabbalistic Numerology.

Master your number
Master your Life

By Kate Rheeders

Master Your Number, Master Your Life is a very comprehensive look at the esoterics of numbers and geometry including Kabbalistic numerology, shadow numbers, the cycles of life, relationship numbers and much more. The author, Kate Rheeders lives and practices in Gauteng, South Africa.

ISBN 0-9584359-5-2

.

22415110R00145

Printed in Great Britain
by Amazon